# Pioneer
# Free Will Baptists
# Ministers
# Burial Locations
# In
# Georgia

## PIONEER FREE WILL BAPTISTS MINISTERS BURIAL LOCATION IN GEORGIA

This book was printed in the United States of America.

To order additional copies of this book, contact:
FWB Publications
Enchanting Acres
1006 Rayme Drive
Columbus, Ohio 43207
Alton.loveless@prodigy.net
Or
www.amazon.com

**FWB**
FWB Publications

## Introduction

## Georgia

This book represents all that were part of the Free Will Baptist movement, consisting of the Palmer (south), Randall (north) and others such as the Stone, John-Thomas, John Wheeler Assns., NC OFWB and more.

Many of the photos are poor quality, but it was all I could find. Likewise, I do not have photos or tombstones for many of them. The information about these ministers were all that was available to me or found in archives. I made every effort to include those for which they would be remembered. Some I had no information, but research had shown they were of our denomination.

This Section is taken for a two Volume set done by this author.

# PIONEER FREE WILL BAPTISTS MINISTERS BURIAL LOCATION IN GEORGIA

# Georgia

## William Amos Addison
Birth:
Apr. 14, 1907
Georgia
Death:
Nov. 17, 1977
Seminole County, Georgia
Burial:
Pilgrims Rest Church Cemetery
Colquitt
Miller County, Georgia

He served in the Martin and Little River Conferences according to the minutes of both Q.M's. Son of George M. Addison and Rosa Miller. His wife was Alma Monday (1907 - 1991).

Inscription:
In Heaven There is One Angel More.

## Amos Banks Adams
Birth:
Sep. 13, 1897
Death:
Nov. 12, 1953
Burial:
Satilla Freewill Baptist Church
Cemetery
Hazlehurst
Jeff Davis County,
Georgia

His name appeared in the South Georgia Minutes in 1936 and during 1938-1953. He married Annie Warnock Adams (1904 - 1982).

## Bennie Allen Altman
Birth:
Jan. 20, 1892
Death:
Apr. 18, 1949
Burial:
Pineview Cemetery
Folkston
Charlton County, Georgia

According to South Georgia minutes he served there between 1940-48.He was a son of Marion Altman (1866 - 1946) and Maggie Altman (1860 - 1926) he was married to Mattie Lou Mizell Altman (1896 - 1982).

**John R Amburgey**
Birth:
Apr. 30, 1940
West Virginia
Death:
Aug. 14, 2002
Patmos
Baker County,Georgia
Burial:
Patmos Free Will Baptist Church Cemetery
Patmos,Baker County Georgia

He was licensed to preach in 1979, ordained in 1980, and had served as pastor at Patmos since 1997. Rev. Amburgey, a native of W. VA, and U.S. Army Veteran, was an alumnus of Hillsdale FWB College, and Salem Bible College, Brevard Com. College (FL) and Bethany Theological Seminary in Dothan, AL. He had pastored churches in AL, MS, and FL, before coming to Patmos Church in GA. In addition to his pastoral ministry, Amburgey served on various boards and committees. He was elected Sec'y of Georgia State Board on Camping (1986-'88; 1998-2002). John Amburgey was known as a man with a sense of humor who supported and promoted every phase of denominational work.

**W L Amerson**
Birth:
Oct. 27, 1911
Death:
Feb. 1, 1996
Burial:
Pine Level Freewill Baptist Church Cemetery
Chester
Dodge County,Georgia

He was a Georgia minister serving in the Georgia Union.

**H A Ammons**
Birth:
1845
Death:
1915

Burial:
Memorial Freewill Baptist
Church Cemetery
Surrency
Appling County,Georgia

Early Georgia minister whose record is found in the 1907 South Georgia Minutes. He was a private in the CSA in Company A, 4th Regiment. he was married to Arvenie James Ammons (1848 - 1920.

## Leonard Short Anthony
Birth:
May 28, 1881
Death:
Jan. 19, 1944
Burial:
New Life Freewill Baptist
Church Cemetery

Marion County,Georgia
Active minister whose name appears in the Chattahoochee, Little River, Midway, Union and Georgia Union Minutes.

---

## Rev David J Apperson
Birth
11 Jan 1810
Clarke County, Georgia, Usa
Death
19 Mar 1894 (Aged 84)
Ellaville, Schley County, Georgia, Usa
Burial
Body Lost Or Destroyed, Specifically: Burial Location Lost Or Unknown At This Time

His parents, James and Elizabeth, were from Mecklenburgh County, Va. Both grandfathers were soldiers in the Revolutionary army. Bro. A. united with the Baptist church in 1827 and was a participant in the early efforts to promote liberal views in Georgia. In 1841 he received license to preach, and three years later, was ordained. He ministered to the Corinth and New Prospect churches thirty years, and served the Friendship, Shiloh, Bluff Spring, Bethany, Galilee and Silver Run churches for briefer periods. He also traveled as a home missionary. In 1850 he was elected moderator of the Chattahoochee Association, and was continued in that position until 1881, a sufficient evidence of the esteem of the brethren. He has baptized 1007 converts. Now he is in feeble health, passing an honored old age with his family at Poindexter, Ga. Free Baptist Cyclopaedia, pp. 21-22

**Allen Bruce Ard**
Birth:
Jul. 21, 1877
Death:
Mar. 5, 1966
Burial:
Salem Cemetery
Desser
Seminole County,Georgia

Early minister serving in the Martin Assn. according to their minutes from 1919 to 1964. His name also appears in the Midway Minutes in 1919.

**John Calvin Arnold**
Birth:
Apr. 25, 1886

Death:
May 1, 1943
Burial:
Zion Hill Cemetery
Millwood
Ware County, Georgia
Minister in the Little River Conference.

**Missionary Laura Belle Barnard**
Birth:
Feb. 13, 1907
Death:
Mar. 10, 1992
Burial:
Ebenezer Cemetery,
Glennville,
Tattnall County,Georgia,
Plot: E2

Free Will Baptist educator, missionary, humanitarian was born and reared in Glennville, Georgia. After graduation from high school, she attended South Georgia Teachers College in Statesboro, and then transferred to Columbia Bible College in South Carolina. She graduated from Columbia in 1932 and shortly thereafter she sensed a call to evangelical mission work. In 1935 she was commissioned for mission work in India by the General Conference of Free Will Baptists of the South. That year the General Conference merged with the Cooperative General Association of Free Will Baptists, a group in the Midwest and Southwest, to form the National Association of Free Will Baptists, becoming the first missionary of a newly formed denomination. Barnard began her mission in Kotagiri, South India, in the summer of 1935. She worked among the "untouchables," the lowest class in the Hindu caste system. In the early 1940s she moved back to the United States and served briefly as a teacher at the fledgling Free Will Baptist Bible College in Nashville, Tennessee, but she soon returned to India, where she remained until 1957. Upon completion of her Master's Degree at Columbia Bible College in 1960, she became a Professor of Missions at the Free Will Baptist Bible College, from which she retired in 1972. Barnard wrote a number of books, including *His Name among All Nations* (1946), which is a theology of missions, and *Touching the Untouchables* (1985), her autobiography. Barnard retired to her hometown of Glennville, where she engaged in numerous ministries, including humanitarian aid to Mexican migrant workers.

**William J Barksdale**
Birth:
Mar. 28, 1932
Worth County, Georgia
Death:
Dec. 26, 2014
Tifton
Tift County,Georgia
Burial:
Poulan Cemetery
Poulan
Worth County,Georgia

Rev. Barksdale was born in Worth County on March 28, 1932 to the late Jutson and Mamie Lois Ellis Barksdale. Rev. Barksdale had lived in Tifton since 1987. He was ordained as a minister in November 1965 and retired after 49 years. He was a veteran of the United States Navy having served during the Korean War. Rev. Barksdale was formerly employed with Lawhorne Tire and liked to hunt and fish. He enjoyed visiting people and seeing to the needs of others. Rev. Barksdale was a member of the Corinth Freewill Baptist Church and was affiliated with the Freewill Baptist Association.

**John Nelson Barnes**
Birth:
Sep. 18, 1895
Death:
Sep. 18, 1961
Burial:
Sowhatchee Cemetery, Blakely
Early County, Georgia

# Their Works Do Follow Them.

**Gerald Baxley**
Birth:
Sep. 17, 1943
Dothan
Houston County, Alabama
Death:
Oct. 25, 1995
Jesup
Wayne County, Georgia
Burial:
Omega Cemetery
Baxley
Appling County, Georgia

The 52-year-old minister pastored Surrency Free Will Baptist Church for seven years. Rev. Baxley was ordained to preach in Feb. 1968. His first pastorate was at his home church, Corinth FWB in Midland City, Alabama. During his 27-year ministry, he pastored eight churches in three states--AL, KY, and GA. He was within 10 days of relocating to his ninth pastorate (New Lebanon FWB Church in Tishomingo, MS, when he died. In addition to pastoral work, Baxley was active in local associational outreach. He served as clerk of Alabama Cahaba River Ass'n, and Georgia's So. Georgia Assn. The Alabama Home Missions Board employed him for a time as interim pastor for the mission work in Enterprise.

**John Lewis Batchelor**
Birth:
Sep. 10, 1925
Death:
May 29, 2004
Burial:
Father's Home Church Cemetery
Camilla
Mitchell County, Georgia

Minister in the Martin and Midway Assn's. His wife was Margie Horn Batchelor (1931 - 2013).

## Johnny Ralph Batchelor

Birth:
Aug. 1, 1893
Miller County, Georgia
Death:
Jul. 6, 1962
Mayhaw
Miller County, Georgia
Burial:
White Plains Freewill Baptist
Church Cemetery
Lucile, Early County, Georgia

Minister. Married to Pauline Inez Cooper Batchelor (1889 - 1963) and a son named Bruce Lawton Batchelor (1911 - 1985).

## L R Beach

Birth:
1867
Death:
Jun. 12, 1950
Burial:
Live Oak Freewill Baptist Church
Cemetery
Milford
Baker County, Georgia

He was a minister in the Martin Assn.

## Ed. C. Beers

Birth:
Unknown
New York
Death:
Sep. 18, 1872
Muscogee County, Georgia
Burial:
Rock Baptist Church Cemetery
Cataula
Harris County, Georgia

SPECULATIVE that this individual is buried at Rehoboth (a.k.a. Rock) Baptist Cemetery - he was residing near Cataula at the time of his death and his son is buried at this cemetery. Said to have been of Dutch ancestry. Aged 74 years on the 1870 census, so evidently born about 1796. Married Sarah Unknown, who survived him. In 1854, he was preacher at the Providence Free Will Baptist Church on St. Mary's Road in Muscogee County, Georgia. They appear as Edmund BEARS (74, born in New York, retired tailor) and Sarah BEARS (61, born South Carolina), with William (38, grist miller), Victoria (33, farm hand), Emma (11, at home), James (9), Charles (7), Ida (5), and Clinton (3), as well as John McNEIL (30, farm hand), Mary WELLS (40, at home) and William WELLS (8) in the household. Sarah appears as a widow, aged 75 years, in the 1880 census household of her son, E. W. BEERS in Georgia Militia District #672 (Hamilton District) in Harris County, Georgia."E. C. BEERS KILLED.-- We learn that when the workmen engaged in bridging Standing Boy Creek returned from dinner yesterday, they found the body of E. C. BEERS in the creek. His satchel was on the tressel at the end of the bridge. It is supposed from this fact that he was resting on the bridge and had fallen asleep and fell, and in the fall struck his head against one of the timbers. He was aged about 70 years. He left a wife and son (E. W. BEERS) who lives near Cataula, Harris County. This is in substance that we learned of the sad affair." [Columbus (GA) Sun newspaper, Thursday, 19 SEP 1872, p. 3.]"THE GEORIGA PRESS [news from around the state].

**Ralph J. Bell**
Birth:
Jul. 25, 1924
Death:
Oct. 19, 1967
Burial:
New Enterprise Freewill Baptist
Church Cemetery
Seminole County, Georgia

Member of Midway Conference

**Rev Billy Michael Bevan**
BIRTH
30 Oct 1947
Tuscaloosa County, Alabama,
USA
DEATH
16 Mar 2017 (aged 69)
Dothan, Houston County,
Alabama, USA
BURIAL
Oak Grove Cemetery
Arlington, Calhoun County,
Georgia, USA

Mr. Billy Michael Bevan, age 69, of Ashford, Alabama, passed away at his home. Billy was a graduate of Free Will Baptist Bible College (Welch College). He was the pastor and a member of Eastside Free Will Baptist Church. Billy pastored churches in Georgia, Mississippi, North Carolina, and Alabama. He pastored at Sardis Free Will Baptist Church in Eufaula, Alabama for 13 years. Billy was the past President of the Southeastern Free Will Baptist College in Wendell, North Carolina. Other members of his family were namely; his father,

Rev. Elzo M. Bevan; Rev. Shawn Williams, Rev. Gregory Bevan. A Celebration of life service was conducted at the Sardis Free Will Baptist Church in Eufaula, Alabama with Rev. Dann Patrick and Rev. Jeff Jones officiating.

Sandra Ogletree Bishop

Birth:
August 27, 1949
Tift County, Georgia
Death:
July 18, 2020
Tipton, Georgia
Cremated

Mrs. Sandra Ogletree Bishop, 70, of Tifton, passed away on at her residence. A private memorial service will be held Tuesday at Corinth Freewill Baptist Church.

Mrs. Bishop was born August 27, 1949 in Tift County to Mrs. Julia Faye Franks Ogletree and the late Leonard Ogletree. In addition to her father, she was preceded in death by one brother, Derrick Ogletree. Mrs. Bishop was a member of Corinth Free Will Baptist Church of Tifton and was a Missionary with IM, Inc., formerly Free Will Baptist International Missions. She was a graduate of Tift County High School and Welch College formerly the Free Will Baptist Bible College in Gallatin, Tennessee with a Bachelor's Degree.

**David W Blanton**
Birth:
Jun. 2, 1857
Death:
Nov. 12, 1916
Burial:
New Hope Free Will Baptist
Church Cemetery
Madray Springs
Wayne County,
Georgia

Preacher in the Ogeechee and South Georgia Quarterly Meetings.

### Isaac J. Blanton
Birth:
Feb. 14, 1861
Duplin County,
North Carolina
Death:
Mar. 16, 1926
Surrency
Appling County,Georgia
Burial:
Memorial Freewill Baptist
Church Cemetery
Surrency
Appling County, Georgia

Isaac was born to Joshua Isham BLANTON (b. c1827) and Elizabeth "Bettie" BLAND (marr. 03 Jul 1852 Duplin Co, NC). He was a minister in the Oqeechee and South Georgia Assn's serving from 1903 to 1925 acccording from the minutes of said conferences.

### David Louis Boatright
Birth:
Oct. 29, 1868
Death:
Nov. 14, 1950
Burial:
Lake Cemetery
Metter, Candler County, Georgia

Minister in the Ogeechee Assn. He married Lillian Cornelia Rogers Boatright (1870 - 1924) and they had son Reuben Lloyd Boatright (1894 - 1918).

### Zachariah Taylor Bone
Birth:
Nov. 26, 1848
Butler
Taylor County, Georgia
Death:
Dec. 24, 1909
Butler
Taylor County, Georgia
Burial:
Mount Pisgah Cemetery
Butler, Taylor County, Georgia

He is recorded in the Chattahoochee minutes from 1891 until 1909. He was married to Sarah L. Decker Bone (1823 - 1912).

**Seaborn Bowen**
Birth:
May 29, 1882
Death:
Jul. 11, 1960
Burial:
Sunnyside Cemetery
Pearson
Atkinson County,Georgia

He was a minister and member of the South Georgia Conference.

**Thomas J. Bowen**
Birth:
Jan. 2, 1814
Death:
Nov. 24, 1875
Burial:
Greensboro City Cemetery
Greensboro
Greene County,Georgia

He was an early minister in the Chattahoochee Conference and appears in the minutes of 1842. Lurana H. Bowen (1832 - 1907) was his wife.

**Barney B. Bradley**
Birth:
Jul. 26, 1907
Death:
Jun. 24, 1949
Burial:
Oak Hill CemeteryGriffin
Spalding County,Georgia
Plot: Section B; Block 2

Records show he was a member of the Chattahoochee Assn.

### David Rowan Braswell
Birth:
Jan. 8, 1877
Decatur County, Georgia
Death:
Jul. 1, 1947
Decatur County, Georgia
Burial:
Salem Cemetery,Desser
Seminole County, Georgia

He pastored in the Martin Association. He was married to Perry Lee Alday Braswell (1874 - 1968).

### Benjamin F. Bratcher
Birth:
Apr., 1883
Georgia
Death:
Mar. 11, 1951
Georgia
Burial:
Carters Chapel Cemetery
Bacon County, Georgia

Minutes of the South Georgia record him as a minister from 1907 until 1931, He married twice.(1) Ella "Ellie" Carter, daughter of Jackson and Mary A. Carter. She is supposed to be buried at Fishing Creek in Pierce Co. GA and second to Lula Deen Powell (1915 - 1998).

HENRY E. BRIDGES
MAR. 29, 1903
JULY 13, 1997

### Henry Elmer Bridges
Birth:
Mar. 29, 1903
Death:
Jul. 13, 1997
Burial:
Mount Calvary Baptist Church Cemetery
Cary
Bleckley County, Georgia

COCHRAN--- Services for the Rev. Henry E. Bridges was held in Mount Calvary Baptist Church with burial in the church cemetery. Bridges, 94, died in a Cochran nursing home. The son of the late West and Cindy English Bridges, he was born in Laurens County but lived most of his life in Bleckley County. A Coast Guard veteran, he was retired from Paulk Lumber Company and as minister of Freewill Baptist Church. He was a member of Little Bethel Freewill Baptist Church. FROM: The Macon Telegraph 7-14-1997 Page 6B

### Oscar C. Bridges
Birth:
Feb. 22, 1877
Death:
Apr. 20, 1948
Burial:
Parkhill Cemetery
Columbus
Muscogee County
,Georgia
Plot: Garden 29

Listed in some of the Chattahoochee minutes of 1917-1947. He was married to Bessie Cromer Bridges (1890 - 1959).

### James Edward Brodnax
Birth:
Dec. 11, 1822
Hancock Co. Georgia
Death:
Feb. 28, 1885
Muscogee Co. GA
Burial:
New Providence Baptist Church
Cemetery
Muscogee County, Georgia

Rev. James Edward Broadnax, son of John Travis Brodnax and Hettie (Gordy) Brodnax, with his brothers settled near Columbus, GA, and was pastor of the Free Will Baptist Church where the Broadnax/Brodnax family have their burial plot. One of these brothers, John M. Broadnax, died from accidental wounds received during the War Between the States and is buried at Providence with Irvin near him. (Rev.) James Edward Broadnax m. Martha Watkins [19 August 1847], and they had 7 children. John Travis Broadnax, a veteran of War of 1812. was living in Hancock, Co., Ga., in 1827, where he drew in that land lottery. The goodness and faithfulness of Rev. Jas. E. Broadnax was appreciated by the whole neighborhood where he preached for 35 years." --from "History of Chattahoochee Co. GA, by N.K. Rogers, copyright, 1933.

Inscription on slab:
"Pioneer Free Will Baptist Preacher; Gave the Land to Providence Free Will Baptist Church.

**John Travis Brodnax**
BIRTH
26 Jun 1780
DEATH

28 May 1862 (aged 81)
BURIAL
New Providence Baptist Church Cemetery
Muscogee County, Georgia, USA

His parents were Stephen Edward Brodnax (1750-1840), and Elizabeth Rebecca Danzee (1758-1840).

He married Hettie Hester (Gordy) 6 Feb. 1821, Baldwin, GA. They had several children as 1850 shows.

Early church tradition says that he was Founder of the Freewill Baptist denomination in the State of Georgia, as identified by a great-great-granddaughter in 1985. We know that John T. was in Georgia Land Lotteries in 1805-1807, and they found him living in Hancock Co and Wilkinson County, and was then in Muscogee County at an early date. It is probably that John T. Brodnax had contact with other early ministers, of the United Baptist and Freewill Baptists, Rev. Cyrus White, and Rev. John James, who worked in the early beginnings of the Georgia United and FWB church.

The Brodnax tombstones provide some information regarding their work in the Providence Free Will Baptist Church, along with John T.'s son, Rev. James Edward Brodnax. Rev. James Edward Brodnax's stone states, "Pioneer Free Will Baptist preacher; Gave the land for Providence FWB Church." Nothing in way of information for this church's organization, etc, could be found when a search of this church's records was made a couple decades ago. But the old cemetery list has a notation by his name: "Organizer and first pastor of Providence Freewill Baptist Church, Columbus, GA." More info regarding dates, etc would be welcome from a family member or other researcher.

**Gerald E. Brown**
Birth:
Jan. 9, 1930
Death:
Aug. 14, 2006
Burial:
Cedar Creek Cemetery
Cordele
Crisp County, Georgia

He was a minister in the Georgia Union, Midway, Union, Little River and Chattahoochee conferences from 1895 through 1998. He was a veteran of the Korean War in the United States Army.

**James Earl Bryant**
Birth:
Jun. 8, 1926
Death:
Oct. 6, 2006
Burial:
Little Bethel Freewill Baptist Church
Cochran
Bleckley County, Georgia

He was a member of the Georgia Union Association and his ministry is recorded in its minutes from 1981 until 1999.

### Robert L Burnett
Birth:
Feb. 26, 1883
Death:
Jun. 15, 1934
Burial:
Mount Nebo Primitive Baptist
Church Cemetery
Charing
Taylor County,Georgia

An early Free Will Baptist preacher whose ministry is recorded in the Chattahoochee minutes from 1915 until 1933.

### T. P. Carr
Birth:
Jan. 8, 1845
Death:
Oct. 26, 1909
Burial:
Mount Olive Freewill Baptist
Church Cemetery
Potterville
Taylor County,Georgia

Early minister in the Chattahoochee Association. His name appears in the Chattahoochee minutes in 1889 and in other editions until 1907.

### William N. Carroll
Birth:
Mar. 30, 1866
Death:
Nov. 12, 1906
Burial:
New Providence Baptist Church
Cemetery
Muscogee County, Georgia

Early minister that served in the Chattahoochee Association. His name appears in the minutes of 1908 and 1909.

### J. C. Hubert Carter
Birth:
May 2, 1925
Death:
Oct. 7, 1988
Burial:
Blackshear City Cemetery
Blackshear
Pierce County,Georgia

He ministered in the Little River, Martin, and South Georgia Association's. His name appears in all three of the minutes of these conferences. he was married to Marjorie J. Carter (1925 - ___) .

### T M Carter
Birth:
Apr. 25, 1900
Death:
Dec. 31, 1953
Burial:
Memorial Freewill Baptist
Church Cemetery
Surrency
Appling County,Georgia

He was a minister in the South Georgia conference. His World War I Draft Registration Cards, 1917-1918 Name: Theopheilus Marion Carter County: Appling State: Georgia Birth Date: 25 Apr 1900 Race: White FHL Roll Number: 1556940 Draft Board: His parents were Millard W Carter (1875 - 1940) and Dealphia Edenfield Carter (1879 - 1954).

### Martin Franklin Cason
Birth:
Jun. 15, 1858
Ware County,
Georgia
Death:
Mar. 31, 1939
Bemiss
Lowndes County,
Georgia
Burial:
Royals Cemetery
Kirkland
Atkinson County,Georgia

Martin was a farmer and a minister serving in the South Georgia conference according to the minutes of 1905 and 1907. He is the son of Hillery William Cason and Pheby Walker Cason. He was married three times to Martha Frances Royal Cason (1868 - 1893),Alice Pafford Cason (1863 - 1910) and Emma Jane Smith Cason (1886 - 1955).

**Henry L Catrett**
Birth:
Feb. 9, 1896
Death:
Aug. 2, 1961
Burial:
Colquitt City Cemetery
Colquitt
Miller County,Georgia
He served in the Midway, Georgia Union, and Martin Associations during the period of 1940 through the 1960s. his wife was Nettie S Catrett (1895 - 1959).

**L J (James) Chambless**
Birth:
Feb. 9, 1926
Alabama
Death:
May 30, 1998
Tift County,Georgia
Burial:
Tift Memorial Gardens and Mausoleum
Tifton

Tift County,Georgia
He was a minister in the Little River Association. His parents were Oscar H. Chambless (1898 - 1953) and Lonia Beasley Chambless (1908 - 1968). He was married to Betty Mason Chambless (1934 - 1994) and to this union was born Barbara Franks Chambless (1943 - 2011).

---

**"I See Heaven Open And Jesus On The Right Hand Of God."**

**Edward S. Cheshire**
Birth:
Apr. 20, 1842
Stewart County,Georgia
Death:
Mar. 31, 1926
Burial:
Friendship Cemetery
Hahira
Lowndes County,Georgia

He was an early minister in the Midway Association. He was married to Julia George Cheshire (1844 - 1918).

### W C Coleman
Birth:
May 14, 1880
Death:
Jan. 21, 1959
Burial:
Bethel Free Will Baptist Church
Cemetery
Appling County,Georgia

Early minister serving in the Georgia Union and South Georgia Associations during the periods from 1916 until 1957.

### George W. Collins
Birth:
Apr. 10, 1880
Death:
Mar. 3, 1960
Burial:
Collins-McCullough Cemetery
Emanuel County,Georgia

He was a minister in the Ogeechee and South Georgia Assn's. His wife was Sarah McCullough Collins (1887 - 1964).

### C C Coursey
Birth:
Aug. 2, 1872
Death:
Nov. 3, 1946
Burial:
Lyons City Cemetery
Lyons
Toombs County,Georgia
In the quarterly meeting minutes it revealed that he served as a minister in the South Georgia

conference from 1913 until about 1946.

### William Robert Crawley
Birth:
Jan. 9, 1912
Ben Hill County,Georgia
Death:
Mar. 28, 1990
Peach County,Georgia
Burial:
Sunset Memorial Gardens
Americus
Sumter County,Georgia
His parents were William Asberry Crawley (1882 - 1960) and Lillie Crawley (1888 - 1915) and he was married to Mary P. Lowell Crawley (1916 - 2007).

### R. Paul Creech
Birth:
Oct. 11, 1962,
Durham,
Durham County,
North Carolina
Death:
Sep. 15, 2011,
Macon,
Bibb County,
Georgia
Burial:

Glen Haven Memorial Garden,
Macon,
Bibb County,
Georgia

Free Will Baptist Minister, missionary to Japan from 1987 to 1988, and to the Ivory Coast, West Africa, from 1989 to 1998. He served churches in New Brunswick, Canada and Georgia. He was a member of the Board of International Missions for the National Association of Free Will Baptists.

### Madison Lamar Crook
Birth:
Dec. 20, 1867
Macon County, Georgia
Death:
Jan. 14, 1934
Burial:
Mount Olive Freewill Baptist
Church Cemetery
Potterville
Taylor County, Georgia

Minister in the Chattahoochee Association according to minutes of 1907-1912.

### Gene Autry Cross
Birth:
Mar. 15, 1947
Death:
Dec. 5, 2004
Burial:
Dawn Memorial Park
Decatur
DeKalb County, Georgia

He served in the Oqeechee and Georgia Union conferences.

### Joshua Edward Daniel
Birth:
Jun. 19, 1861
Death:
Aug. 6, 1928
Burial:
Forest Park City Cemetery
Forest Park
Clayton County, Georgia

Early minister in the Middle Georgia association. He was the son of Richard Daniel (1813 - 1891) and Sarah Norman Daniel (1831 - 1897). He was married to Mary J. Daniel (1861 - 1942).

**Willie Dawson**
Birth:
Unknown
Death:
Sep. 12, 2012
Jamieson,Gadsden
County,Florida
Burial:
Cool Springs Cemetery
Faceville, Decatur County,
Georgia

He served churches in Florida and Georgia living to the age of 76 dying at his home in Jamieson, Florida. He served as a deacon at the First Free Will Baptist church in Quincy, Florida and after his call to the ministry served as a bi-vocational preacher. By trade he was a construction worker. His last church was the First FWB in Bainbridge, Ga. He gave sacrificially to both home and international missions because missionary Sandra Payne was his sister.

**G Thomas Dell**
Birth:
Aug. 17, 1872
Death:
Mar. 10, 1956
Burial:
Wesley Chapel Methodist
Church Cemetery
Berlin
Colquitt County,Georgia

Minister in the Union Assn.

**Damon C. Dodd**
Birth:
Feb. 14, 1916,
Flat River,
St. Francois County, Missouri
Death:
Apr. 27, 2000,
Colquitt, Miller County,Georgia
Burial:
Donley, Bellview,
Miller County,Georgia

Free Will Baptist leader, pastor, and missionary. Bro. Dodd was converted at the age of 15 during an evangelistic crusade by the McAdams Evangelistic Team. The speaker on that blessed, fateful evening was a woman, Lizzie McAdams. He was ordained into the Gospel Ministry in 1936 at the St. Francois County Quarterly meeting in Missouri. Damon married Sylvia R. Wood in 1938, and God gave them two lovely girls and fifty-eight years of companionship and service together.

Sylvia's roots came from Joshua Wood who was one of three Wood families that came to St. Francois County Missouri from Ohio near 1866. They started most of the Free Will Baptist churches in the area. Damon attended Flat River Jr. College, but when the Free Will Baptist Bible College began in 1942. He and his wife, Sylvia, joined seven other students. Two years later they made up half of the first graduating class. Brother Dodd went on with his formal education until he received a Doctor of Ministries degree in the 1980s. Study was a joy and writing was a passion for him. He wrote as he spoke, with enthusiasm. He published, *All of Mine For Him*, 1954, *The Free Will Baptist Story*, 1956; *Go Home Tell Thy Friends*, 1957; *Trailways to Adventure, 1963; Study Guide for Revelation, 1967; Handbook for New Church Members,* 1970;

*Marching Through Georgia,* 1977.

Damon and Sylvia were foreign missionaries to Cuba, 1945-48. He served as the fourth National Association Executive-Secretary, 1949-53. In 1953 he was the first full-time Promotional Secretary for the National Home Missions Dept. and opened its first national office. Damon was a Foreign Missions Board Member, 1944-46, and a Free Will Baptist Bible College Trustee Board Member, 1962-76.

In Georgia, Brother Dodd served as: the State Moderator; the state's Historical Commission; Chairman of the Committee that wrote the Standard and Doctrinal Examination for Licensing and Ordaining Free Will Baptist Ministers in Georgia, which was adopted by the state association, November 16, 1979. He served as an evangelist, church planter and pastor.

He served churches in Missouri, 1937-42, 1947-50; Tennessee, 1942-46; and in Georgia. His first Georgia pastorate was in Savannah, 1958-62, South Georgia Association. Later he served the congregations at Homerville, 1965-73, Little River Association; Bay, 1974-75, Union Association; New Home, Miller County, 1975-81 and 90, Martin Association; Bellview, 1983 and 1987, Midway Association.

## Missionary Sylvia *Wood* Dodd

Birth:
Jan. 25, 1917,
Missouri
Death:
May 5, 1996,
Colquitt, Miller County,Georgia
Burial:
Donley Cemetery,Colquitt,
Miller County,Georgia

She traveled with Texas woman preacher, Lizzie McAdams, playing the piano in her evangelistic ministry. Damon Dodd had been converted in her revival in Missouri. Lizzie was unhappy to lose her to Damon, but concluded that she'd be a blessing to Damon in his ministry. Sylvia's roots came from Joshua Wood who was one of three Wood families that came to St. Francois County Missouri from Ohio near 1866. They started most of the Free Will Baptist churches in the area. It is the oldest conference in the state of Missouri and contains many churches in the lead belt section of the state.

**E Allen Drake**

Birth:
Aug. 1, 1864
Death:
Jan. 18, 1946
Burial:
Corinth Cemetery
Iron City
Seminole County,Georgia

According to the Martin conference minutes he served from 1902 until about 1943. he was married to Sallie W. Drake (1871 - 1962).

**W A Drake**

Birth:
1858
Death:
1930
Georgia
Burial:
Finch Cemetery
Philomath
Oglethorpe County,Georgia

He was an early minister serving in the Martin Association according records from1919 and 1921.

**William S Driggers**

Birth:

Apr. 1, 1910
Death:
May 31, 1987
Burial:
Mount Gilead Freewill Baptist
Church Cemetery
Decatur County,Georgia
As a minister he served in the South Georgia, Chattahoochee, Midway and Martin Associations.

Inscription:
TEC 5 US ARMY WWII

### Earl B Duckworth
Birth:
Apr. 18, 1905
Death:
Oct. 11, 1989
Burial:
Glen Haven Memorial Garden
Macon
Bibb County,Georgia
Plot: Everlasting Life 163 D # 3

According to the South Georgia and Georgia Union minutes he served as a minister from about 1935 to 1988 in both of these conferences.

### Harold Keith Dunlap
Birth:
Nov. 3, 1926
Death:
Feb. 1, 1999
Burial:
Macon Memorial Park
Macon, Bibb County,Georgia

He was a member of the Georgia Union Conference according to its minutes from 1967 until 1979 his record appears.

### James M Dunn
Birth:
Mar. 5, 1856
Georgia
Death:
1929
Georgia
Burial:
Bay Springs Free Will Baptist
Church Cemetery
Plainfield
Dodge County,
Georgia

The Georgia Union of minutes show him serving as a clergyman in their 1925 through 1927 records. He was married to Isabella Jones Dunn (1875 -

1923) to whose union was born Joseph T Dunn (1914 - 1987).

### J H Dupree
Birth:
Nov. 29, 1846
Death:
Jun. 12, 1922
Burial:
New Prospect Freewill Baptist
Coverdale
Turner County, Georgia

According to the Chattahoochee minutes he ministered within the Association from 1879 until 1913. He also served in the Confederate States of America Army.
Inscription:
Co C 55 GA INF
Confederate States Army

### James Thomas Edwards
Birth:
Jan. 23, 1876
Baker County, Georgia
Death:
May 28, 1964
Baker County, Georgia
Burial:
Travelers Rest Freewill Baptist
Church Cemetery
Newton
Baker County, Georgia
He was a minister in the Martin conference. He was married to Rossie Bailey Edwards (1880 - 1964).

### Adolphus Emanuel
Birth:
Oct. 29, 1868
Cumberland County, North
Carolina
Death:

Sep. 18, 1948
Emanuel County, Georgia
Burial:
Collins Cemetery
Oak Park
Emanuel County, Georgia

Named as one of the ministers in the promotion and organization of the GA Free Will Bapt. State Association in 1917.

### John M Emanuel
Birth:
Sep. 24, 1875
Death:
Aug. 24, 1943
Burial:
Cool Spring Cemetery
Candler County,
Georgia

He served as a minister in the Chattahoochee, Midway and South Georgia conferences from 1906 until about 1942.

### George Troup Embry
Birth:
Dec. 4, 1832
Death:
Apr. 11, 1916
Burial:
Morgan Methodist Church
Cemetery
Morgan
Calhoun County,
Georgia

He was the son of Hezekiah Luckie Embry and Martha Slaton Lowe. He was an early minister in the Liberty and Martin

Associations 1892 through 1894. He was married to Sarah Elizabeth Wolfe Embry (1834 - 1906) and they had one child Nancy E Embry (1854 - 1890).

### Elder William H. Emerson
Birth:
Mar. 26, 1876
Georgia
Death:
Aug. 16, 1948
Macon County, Georgia
Burial:
Little Bethel Freewill Baptist
Cemetery
Ideal
Macon County, Georgia

Minutes show that he appeared as a minister from 1903 until 1948 in the Chattahoochee, Georgia Union and Midway Associations.

### Charles B Ethridge
Birth:
May 1, 1886
Death:
Jul. 13, 1929

Burial:
Underwood Memorial Cemetery
Conyers
Rockdale County, Georgia

He served as a minister in the Chattahoochee and Georgia are Union Associations. He was married to Ludie Mae Ethridge (1891 - 1969).

**Grady C Etheredge, Sr**
Birth:
Apr. 14, 1910
Death:
Dec. 28, 1975
Burial:
Live Oak Freewill Baptist Church
Cemetery
Milford
Baker County, Georgia

He was a minister in the Chattahoochee Association.

**Alton Everson**
Birth:
Sep. 4, 1922
Death:
Feb. 7, 1988
Burial:
Colquitt City Cemetery

Colquitt
Miller County, Georgia

His combined ministry was in the Little River, Georgia Union, South Georgia, Union, and an Martin associations.

**Death Is The Fundamental Human Problem.**

**Howard Dewitt Faircloth**
Birth:
Jan. 5, 1924
Dodge County,
Georgia
Death:
Oct. 24, 2014
Dublin
Laurens County,
Georgia
Burial:

Bay Springs
Free Will Baptist Church
Cemetery
Plainfield
Dodge County
Georgia

Rev. Howard Faircloth, age 90, of Eastman died at Carl Vincent Medical Center.

Rev Faircloth was a member of Bay Springs Freewill Baptist Church where he served as pastor for twenty-five years and a total of fifty-six years in various churches. He was also retired from Robins Air Force Base and a veteran of WW II.

Rev. Faison died at age 55 in Millen, Georgia after a long illness. He was a native of Moultrie, Georgia and pastor of the Deep Creek Free Will Baptist Church in Millen. He was a pastor and lifelong Free Will Baptist. The Reverends James Ussery, Larry Dale Williams, and Galen Dunbar officiated at his service.

**Kenneth L. Faison**
Birth:
May 23, 1935
Death:
Jul. 19, 1990
Burial:
Glennville City Cemetery
Glennville, Tattnall County,
Georgia
Plot: D5

**Hoyt Duard Finley**
Birth:
Sep. 21, 1920
Death:
Sep. 19, 1989
Hart County, Georgia
Burial:
Poplar Springs Baptist Church
Cemetery
Lavonia
Franklin County,Georgia

He was a minister in the Georgia Union and Chattahoochee Associations during a period of around 1954 through 1992. He was a S SGT US ARMY in WWII where he received a Purple Heart.

**Joseph Otis Fort**
Birth:
May 2, 1910,
Early County, Georgia
Death:
Mar. 7, 1976,
Early County, Georgia
Burial:
Jakin Freewill Baptist Church Cemetery,
Jakin, Early County, Georgia

He was a minister in three of the Georgia associations, namely; Midway, South Georgia and Martin. His name appears in nearly all of the minutes beginning as early as 1933 until 1968.

**Drew Floyd**
Birth:
Sep. 5, 1882
Miller County, Georgia
Death:
Mar., 1971

Miller County, Georgia
Burial:
Rawls Cemetery
Colquitt
Miller County, Georgia

He was a minister in the Martin Association where records show he served from 1943 until about 1969. First wife: Eula Inez Pickren. Second wife: Linda Grimes Powell. Son of Thomas Newton Floyd and Eliza Rawls Floyd.

**Herschel Greeley Fowler**
Birth:
Nov. 8, 1888
Death:
Jul. 20, 1981
Burial:
Bethlehem Baptist Church Cemetery
Condor, Laurens County, Georgia

He is listed as a minister in the Chattahoochee minutes.

**Elder Harvey W Giddens**
Birth:
Jul. 12, 1909
Death:
Apr. 14, 1981
Burial:
Bridge Creek Cemetery
Colquitt County, Georgia

During his ministry he served in the Chattahoochee, Little River and Georgia Union Associations.

**Murray Elvin Giddens**
Birth:
Nov. 15, 1930

Adel
Cook County, Georgia
Death:
Jan. 3, 2009
Moultrie
Colquitt County, Georgia
Burial:
Suncrest Memorial Gardens
Moultrie, Colquitt County,
Georgia

The course of his ministry was spent in the Union, Little River, and Martin Association's from about 1974 until 1990. A veteran, he was retired from the Marines and was a Free Will Baptist minister. In addition to his parents, He was preceded in death by his wife, Myrtice Foster Giddens.

---

### Teedom M. Giddens
Birth:
Aug. 23, 1891
Coffee County, GA
Death:
Oct. 19, 1961
Burial:
Sunnyside Cemetery
Pearson
Atkinson County,Georgia

His ministry was confined to the Little River Association. Spouse: Beadie Mae Burch. Married: Abt. 1914 in Georgia and his parents were. Kindred Jasper Giddens (1861 - 1938) and Martha Lewis Giddens (1871 - 1954) and he married Beadie Mae Burch Giddens (1891 - 1972).

---

### Chester A Gilbert
Birth:
Oct. 4, 1898
Death:
Feb. 12, 1977
Burial:
New Salem Cemetery
Miller County, Georgia

His ministry spanned from 1943 until 1969 in the Martin Association. Spouse: Ida Jane Nobles Gilbert (1902-36).

---

### Benjamin Terrell Gill
Birth:
Jan. 2, 1890
Death:
Oct. 30, 1972
Burial:
Trinity Freewill Baptist Cemetery
Taylor County,Georgia

His ministry was held in the Chattahoochee Association and he is recorded in its minutes from about 1934 until 1971.

---

### Walter D Gill
Birth:
Oct. 9, 1866
Death:
Apr. 18, 1934
Burial:
Trinity Freewill Baptist
Cemetery
Taylor County,Georgia

His ministry appears in many of the minutes of the Chattahoochee Association ranging from 1903 until 1933.

### Richard Harold Goolsby
Birth:
Jul., 1855
Jasper County, Georgia
Death:
Mar. 16, 1935
Monticello
Jasper County, Georgia
Burial:
Hebron Cemetery
Jasper County, Georgia

Records in 1897 show him as a minister in the Middle Georgia minutes.

### William Hancil Gray
Birth:
Mar. 9, 1915
Death:
Apr. 16, 1995
B
urial:
Chastain Memorial Park
Cemetery
Blue Ridge
Fannin County,
Georgia

He was a minister in the Georgia Union association.

### Benjamin Franklin Green
Birth:
1873
Monroe County,Georgia
Death:
1938
Marion County,Georgia
Burial:

New Life Freewill Baptist
Church Cemetery
Marion County, Georgia

His parents were Thomas C Green (1824- ) and Irena M (Helton) (1836- ).He married Lucy Bone on Nov 17, 1892 in Taylor Co, GA. He was a minister in the union conference.

**Doctor Evan Green**
Birth:
Oct. 5, 1852
Death:
Jul. 6, 1936
Ideal
Macon County, Georgia
Burial:
Ideal City Cemetery
Ideal
Macon County, Georgia

Macon County Citizen-Montezuma Georgian July 9, 1936. Ideal, Ga. - July 8, Funeral services were held in the Free Will Baptist Church in Ideal Tuesday afternoon for Rev. D. E. Greene, 83, prominent minister and former postmaster of Ideal, whose death occurred at his home Monday following a lingering illness. Rev. Greene was the first citizen who moved to the town of Ideal and was postmaster here from the founding of the town until two years ago. For many years he walked and carried the mail from Oglethorpe to Ideal, a distance of 15 miles, until the A. B. C. Railroad was built, connecting these points. For 40 years he was a minister in the Free Will Baptist Church and served many charges. He was married to Miss Frances Dyson who died in 1922.

**Benjamin J. Griffin**
Birth:
Jul. 26, 1849
Death:
Mar. 25, 1926
Burial:
Leila Cemetery
Colquitt County, Georgia,

The Liberty minutes show him as early as 1895 as a minister in the Association.

Death Is The Fundamental Human Problem.

**E C Grimsley**
Birth:
Apr. 29, 1859
Death:
May 3, 1939
Burial:

New Life Freewill Baptist
Church Cemetery
Marion County, Georgia

The Chattahoochee minutes revealed that he appeared in their conference from 1898 until 1938.

**William Thomas Grimsley**
Birth:
Apr., 1879
Georgia
Death:
Oct. 20, 1942
Marion County, Georgia
Burial:
Parmer Cemetery
Oakland
Marion County, Georgia
He served as a minister in the Chattahoochee Association whose minutes revealed his presence from 1919 until 1942.

**Claud H Hadden**
Birth:
Jul. 12, 1890
Death:
Oct. 11, 1970
Burial:
Lake Cemetery
Metter

Candler County, Georgia

He served in the Ogeechee and South Georgia Quarterly Meetings from about 1940 untill 1960.

### C W Harrell
Birth:
Oct. 13, 1943
Death:
Oct. 18, 1992
Burial:
Mizpah Primitive Baptist Church Cemetery
Cairo
Grady County, Georgia

He was a minister in both the Union and Martin Associations.

**The Lord Has Prepared For His Warriors**

### Kelly C Harrell
Birth:
Jan. 28, 1934
Death:
Apr. 16, 1997
Burial:
Mount Gilead Freewill Baptist Church Cemetery
Decatur County, Georgia

He served as a minister in the Martin Association.

Inscription:
AMN US AIR FORCE KOREA

### James G Harris
Birth:
Sep. 7, 1883
Death:
Nov. 3, 1926
Burial:
Christ Methodist Church Cemetery
Baker County, Georgia

Minutes from the Martin and Midway Associations revealed him as a minister from 1916 until 1926 within their associations.

### C J Harvey
Birth:
Jan. 6, 1889
Death:
Aug. 2, 1960
Burial:
Oakview Cemetery
Camilla
Mitchell County, Georgia

He was a minister in the Georgia Union, the Midway, and Union conferences during the period of 1929 until 1959.

### R Slaten Hayes
Birth:
May 28, 1913
Death:
Nov. 9, 2002
Burial:
Forest Hill Freewill Baptist
Church Cemetery
Adel
Cook County, Georgia

From 1952 until 1999 he served as a minister in the Little River and Union Associations.

### Bessie *Widener* Hillis
Birth
April 23, 1890
Death
July 9, 1969
Burke County, Georgia
Burial
Corinth Cemetery
Burke County, Georgia

She was an early Free Will Baptist preacher in Georgia.

### Joel I Hill
Birth:
Apr. 13, 1851
Early County, Georgia
Death:
May 10, 1914
Early County, Georgia
Burial:
Springfield Baptist Church
Cemetery
Early County
Georgia

He was converted in 1872 and two year's later and received license to preach. He was ordained in 1875 by J. B. McCullers and others. He ministered to the Howard's Grove church, Alabama; New Salem church, Georgia, and the Springfield church, Georgia.

### Robert W Holmes
Birth:
Jun. 2, 1899
Death:
Oct. 12, 1976
Burial:
Pelham City Cemetery
Pelham
Mitchell County, Georgia

He was a minister in the Martin conference.

### W. H. Holmes
Birth:
Jun. 10, 1870
Death:
Jun. 10, 1925
Burial:
Pine Level Church Cemetery
Alma
Bacon County, Georgia

Records in the Chattahoochee, the Georgia Union, and South Georgia minutes revealed his ministry among them from 1902 until 1924.

### George Sherrod Holton
Birth:
Oct. 9, 1909
Death:
Unknown
Burial:
Mount Zion Church Cemetery
Lyons
Toombs County
Georgia
He served in the South Georgia and Ogeechee Associations ranging from about 1952 until 1995.

### Benjamin Franklin Horne
Birth:
Sep., 1866
Laurens County
Georgia
Death:
Oct. 6, 1944
Dodge County
Georgia
Burial:
Bay Springs
Free Will Baptist Church
Cemetery
Plainfield
Dodge County
Georgia

The Georgia Union minutes record him from 1914 until 1943. He was married to Maryann Francis Jones Horne (1867 - 1934) and they had the following children: Joseph William Horne (1890 - 1967) John Benjamin Jefferson Horne (1896 - 1965) Charlton James Horne (1898 - 1985) Henry H Horne (1904 - 1958) Seaborn Horne (1905 - 1905) Athie Belle Horne Graham (1906 - 1947) Fannie C Horne Rodgers (1909 - 1999).

### Carlton Robert Houston
Birth:
May 7, 1914
Death:
Aug. 10, 1983
Burial:
Roberts Cemetery
Miller County, Georgia

He served as a minister in the Martin and, Midway Associations.

### Dennis Oliver Irvin
Birth:
Oct. 25, 1926
Death:
Jun. 13, 1981
Burial:
Travelers Rest Freewill Baptist Church Cemetery
Newton, Baker County, Georgia
His ministry was in the Midway and Union Associations.

### Paul H Irvin
Birth:
Nov. 25, 1925
Baker County,
Georgia
Death:
Dec. 2, 2008
Albany
Dougherty County,
Georgia
Burial:
Travelers Rest Freewill Baptist
Church Cemetery
Newton
Baker County, Georgia

He had a broad ministry serving in the Georgia Union, Midway, Union, and Martin Associations. He was a member of Travelers Rest Free Will Baptist Church. Rev. Irvin had pastored 12 churches in the past 47 years. He was preceded in death by four brothers, Herman Irvin, Price Irvin, Dennis Irvin and Lawrence Irvin,

### Von Deron Irvin
Birth:
Jul. 14, 1910
Death:
Dec. 9, 1985
Burial:
Travelers Rest Freewill Baptist
Church Cemetery
Newton
Baker County, Georgia

His ministry was in two associations: the Midway and Chattahoochee Quarterly Meetings.

### Arthur D Ivey, Sr
BIRTH 1882
DEATH 1960 (aged 77–78)
BURIAL
Hodges Cemetery
Jakin, Early County, Georgia

### John Pierce James
Birth:
Sep. 2, 1809
Rockingham County,
North Carolina
Death:
Oct. 9, 1847
Burial:
Sardis Baptist Church Cemetery
McDonough
Henry County, Georgia

John professed conversion at the age of twenty-four, and was baptized by Rev. Cyrus White at Teman church, Henry County, Georgia. He was subsequently ordained to the gospel ministry at said church in 1835, by what presbytery the author is not informed. Though his ministry was thus commenced under those who were known as Whiteites, (and who were deemed as rather Arminian in sentiment,). He subsequently connected himself with the Central Association, in which body he was highly esteemed and eminently useful.

He was engaged in the ministry only about twelve years, yet he baptized about sixteen hundred persons. His labors were confined mostly to the counties of Jasper, Butts, Henry, Newton and Campbell. His burning zeal impelled him forward day and night, summer and winter. His first sermon was preached under a bush-arbor in Gwinnett County, and from that day until he ceased from his labors was his voice heard in the highways and hedges, inviting and urging the poor and needy to come to the gospel feast. It was by no means an uncommon thing with him to work hard on his farm all day, and, leaving his horse to rest, to walk from three to four miles and preach to his neighbors at night, after which he would return home, and resume his work in the morning. His last sermon was preached at Enon church, Jasper County, from Acts xx. 32: "And now, brethren, I commend you to God," etc.

In October, 1830, he was married to Miss Nancy Strickland, daughter of Colonel Solomon Strickland, of Henry county, who proved herself eminently qualified for the position she was called to occupy as a preacher's wife, and as the mother of six orphan children, which were left upon her hands by his death. His father, Martin James, was a soldier in the war of 1812, was taken prisoner, and died at Fort Johnson. His mother's maiden name was Martha Woodall. She died in 1869, in the ninetieth year of her age.

**John H Jenkins**
Birth:
Aug. 26, 1869
Georgia
Death:
Aug. 10, 1899,
Burial:
Sand Hill Cemetery
Fort Stewart
Tattnall County, Georgia
His name is recorded as a minister in the 1890s minutes of the Chattahoochee Association.

**G W Jones**
Birth:
Aug. 22, 1877
Death:
Jun. 23, 1938
Burial:
Satilla Freewill Baptist Church
Cemetery
Hazlehurst
Jeff Davis County, Georgia

Minutes from the South Georgia conference revealed him serving in their area from their minutes dated 1916 until 1937.

**Spurgeon Jones**
Birth:
Dec. 22, 1914
Death:
May 29, 1970
Burial:
Mt. Ararat Free Will Baptist
Church
Chauncey
Dodge County
Georgia

He preached in the Georgia
Union conference.

---

**Dr. Linton C. Johnson**
Birth:
Feb. 3, 1914,
Alma,
Bacon County
Georgia
Death:
Jun. 26, 2002,
Norfolk, Norfolk City,
Virginia
Burial:
Pine Level Church Cemetery,
Alma, Bacon County,
Georgia

He was a Free Will Baptist
minister, pastor, educator and
Bible college president. He
attended Middle Georgia College,
1932-33 and earned his degree
from Bob Jones College in 1939.
He pursued graduate studies at
Winona Lake School of Theology
in 1943, and Bob Jones Graduate
School in 1945.

Bob Jones University bestowed
the honorary Doctor of
Humanities degree on him in
1952.

He was the founding president of
Free Will Baptist Bible College in
Nashville, Tennessee in 1942,
where he served for 34 years
until his retirement in 1979.
From 1979 until 1981 he was
Chancellor of the college. His
pastorates included Free Will
Baptist churches in Georgia,
Mississippi, Florida and
Tennessee.

He considered the Free Will
Baptist Bible College his great life
work and never allowed
anything to distract him from
that focus. As the president of the
college, Johnson became well

known and respected in academic circles.

He was listed in Who's Who in American College and University Administrations, served on Executive Committee of the American Association of Bible Colleges, participated on the program of the 1976 World Congress of Fundamentalists in Edinburg, Scotland and was a member of the over view committee for the New King James Version of the Bible.

Dr. Johnson preached six times in the national convention and was elected as moderator of the National Association of Free Will Baptist twice. His influence marked the denomination for almost 70 years. In a 1999 tribute, Dr. Robert Picirilli wrote of him, "When the history of Free Will Baptists in the last half of the 20th century is written, the role of Dr. L.C. Johnson will be perhaps the most prominent of any,"

No one as touched more lives within the Free Will Baptist denomination.

**Rev Edmond Barnebus Joyner**
BIRTH

11 Apr 1879
Georgia, USA
DEATH
25 Jun 1960 (aged 81)
BURIAL
Rose Hill Cemetery
Alma, Bacon County, Georgia

Rev. Edmond B. Joyner was an ordained Free Will Baptist minister and was pastor in South Carolina, Georgia, his native state, and in Florida. He registered as a minister in the Eastern General Association of FWB in 1936 when it met in Glennville, GA.

**Hughie J. Kelly**
Birth:
Feb. 16, 1907
Death:
Jul. 20, 1957
Burial:
Evergreen Memory Gardens
Cemetery,
Columbus,
Muscogee County,
Georgia,
Plot: Christus Garden

His ministry was in the Chattahoochee Association..

### Hiram Leroy Knighton
Birth:
Jul. 20, 1906
Georgia
Death:
Jul. 31, 1984
Albany
Dougherty County, Georgia
Burial:
Parkhill Cemetery
Columbus
Muscogee County, Georgia
Plot: Section I-30

Hiram Leroy Knighton was first married to Mary Elizabeth Hearn and upon her death in 1939 married Sarah (Harrell) Knighton. His ministry was in the Chattahoochee and Midway Associations.

### William Berrien Wesley Lane
Birth:
Jan. 24, 1854
Early County, Georgia
Death:
Mar. 5, 1893
Early County, Georgia
Burial:
Sowhatchee Cemetery
Blakely, Early County, Georgia

An early minister in the Chattahoochee and Martin Associations and is recorded in their minutes beginning in 1981 until 1892. He was the husband of Margaret J. (Anglin) Lane and son of Joseph William Lane, III and Chloe Elizabeth (Sheffield) Lane. He was converted in 1870, received license to preach in 1879, and was ordained the following year by Rev. C. C. Martin and J. E. Hill. His ministry was spent in the Chattahoochee Association, Georgia, where he baptized 125 converts organized two churches and aided in the gathering of three others.

### Greenville L. Laney
Birth:
Mar. 5, 1941
Death:
Nov. 15, 1983
Burial:
Riverdale Cemetery
Columbus
Muscogee County, Georgia
Plot: 80 Sec. 10

His ministry was in the Chattahoochee Association.

### Simeon Roy Lawhorn
Birth:
Feb. 23, 1879
Death:
Aug. 16, 1935
Burial:
New Providence Baptist
Cemetery
Marion County, Georgia

He was a minister in the Chattahoochee Association whose minutes show him from 1921 until 1934.

### William Randolph Lawhorn
Birth:
Jun. 10, 1883
Death:
Feb. 8, 1971
Burial:
Sand Bethel Cemetery
Rupert
Taylor County, Georgia

He was the son of William H "W H" Lawhorn (1853 - 1897) and the husband of Effie Alberta "Berta" Watson Lawhorn (1884 - 1961). He was a member the Chattahoochee Association where the minutes revealed that he was active from 1918 until 1970.

**Bruce V Lisle**
Birth:
1901
Death:
1952
Burial:
Parkhill Cemetery
Columbus
Muscogee County, Georgia
Plot: Section F

He was a minister in the Chattahoochee Association.

**Ralph Lightsey**
Birth:
1918
Appling County, Georgia
Death:
Sep. 2, 2012
Statesboro, Bulloch County, Georgia
Burial:
Eastside Cemetery, Statesboro, Bulloch County, Georgia

Dr. Lightsey received his A.B. degree from Mercer University in 1945, a B.D. degree in Theology from Emory University in 1951, a Master's in Theology from Columbia University in 1955 and a doctorate degree in Education from the University of Georgia in 1965. He was ordained to the gospel ministry in 1940. He served churches in Georgia, Alabama, North Carolina and Mississippi. After serving as an active pastor for more than 52 years, he served as a supply speaker at more than 50 churches in Bulloch and surrounding counties. In addition, he was an educator. He served 16 years as professor of Educational Research at Georgia Southern University and as an assistant to the vice-president. Upon his retirement, the Board of Regents conferred on him the title of Professor Emeritus of Educational Research. In keeping with his concern for his fellow human being, he received the Dean Day Smith Service to Mankind Award. He was also the original owner of Lightsey Construction Company, Inc.

**Tom Joseph Lightsey**
Birth:
Jun. 24, 1929
Appling County
Georgia
Death:
Jan. 25, 2010
Palm Garden Rehabilitation Center
Jacksonville
Duval Co. Florida
Burial:
Piney Grove Free Will Baptist Church Cemetery
Appling County, Georgia

He was a member of the Piney Grove Free Will Baptist Church

and was an ordained Free Will Baptist minister. He served several churches as pastor in Southeast Georgia including Alabaha Free Will Baptist in Pierce County. After teaching for several years in the public school system, he completed his career at West Georgia University in Carrollton, from which he retired. Rev. Dr. Charles Thigpen and the Rev. Steve Hughes officiated. According to the South Georgia minutes he is recorded from 1956 through 1998 as a minister.

## James D. Little
Birth:
Mar. 3, 1875
Death:
Aug. 16, 1958
Burial:
Sunnyside Cemetery Pearson
Atkinson County Georgia

Minutes of the Chattahoochee, Georgia Union and Little River associations from 1910 through 1957 record him as a minister.

## S. N. Little
Birth:
Apr. 3, 1848
Death:
Mar. 3, 1932
Burial:
New Prospect Freewill Baptist
Coverdale
Turner County, Georgia

He was an early Free Will Baptist preacher in Georgia.

## Theron Wyndell Long
Birth:
Nov. 24, 1935
Death:
Aug. 1, 2011
Coffee Regional Medical Center,
Burial:
Surrency Cemetery
Surrency
Appling County, Georgia

Rev. Long, a former Free Will Baptist minister and a native of Appling County, was a Southern Baptist Minister for many years. He was an Alumnus of the

Freewill Baptist College of Nashville, Tennessee. He was the son of the late Doric Quitman Long and the late Ola Evelyn Carter Long. He was also preceded in death by a brother, Wyndell Long. Funeral Services were held at the College Avenue Baptist Church, with Rev. Don Harper, Rev. Luther Burns, and Rev. J. E. Blanton officiating.

### James B Lovering
Birth:
Feb. 7, 1912
Death:
Dec. 4, 1976
Burial:
Colquitt City Cemetery
Colquitt
Miller County, Georgia

He was a minister in the Midway, Martin, Little River, and George Union associations recorded as early as 1940 until 1963 in their minutes. Spouse: Flora Newsom Lovering (1915 - 1997).

### L O Lovett
Birth:
Mar. 9, 1882
Death:
May 10, 1965
Burial:
Pine Grove Baptist Church
Cemetery
Nashville
Berrien County, Georgia

He was a minister in the Union Association.

### J W Loyless

Birth:
Jan. 6, 1907
Death:
Feb. 21, 1976
Burial:
Oak City Cemetery
Bainbridge
Decatur County, Georgia

He was a minister in the Midway Association.

### Henry Lewis Lumpkin

Birth:
Mar. 9, 1878
Talbot County, Georgia
Death:
Dec. 26, 1946
Taylor County
Georgia
Burial:
Pine Level Cemetery
Mauk
Taylor County, Georgia

He married Emma Virginia Whitley in Talbot County on July 28, 1897. His parents were William J. and Sarah Lumpkin and he was the grandson of J.L and Jane (Hancock) Lumpkin. He was called to preach at the age of 18. He served in the Free Will Baptists denomination. He was a member of Woodmen of the World. He was the father of seven children. His two sons, William Robert and John Beverly were well known preachers. Henry and his two sons, William Robert and John Beverly all at some time were Pastors at New Life Church. During his ministry he preached in the Chattahoochee, Georgia Union and South Georgia conferences from about 1903 till 1942.

### Johnnie Beverly Lumpkin

Birth:
Oct. 29, 1906
Georgia
Death:
Jan. 30, 2002
Georgia,
Burial:
Pine Level Cemetery
Mauk
Taylor County,
Georgia

Husband of Blanche Hart Lumpkin. He was the son of Henry L. Lumpkin and Emma Watson Lumpkin. During his ministry he preached in the Chattahoochee, Georgia Union, Little River, Union, and Martin associations.

**William Robert Lumpkin, Sr**
Birth:
Aug. 19, 1904
Taylor County, Georgia
Death:
Jun. 13, 1991
Blountsville
Blount County, Alabama
Burial:
Pine Level Cemetery
Mauk, Taylor County, Georgia

W.R., attended Mauk and Berry High School. He worked with Goodrich in Silvertown, Thomaston, Georgia. He was raised on a farm. He was a Mason in the late 1920's and early 1930's. He was a member of Woodmen of the World. He was saved in his bedroom in 1938. He was called to preach the Gospel and pastored several churches including; New Life in Talbot County, Spring Hill in Marion County, Trinity in Charing, Eastman in Dodge County, Cloud Springs in Ft. Oglethorpe, Temple in Rossville and Ft. Perry in Taylor County. He was married to Leila Foster on January 2, 1927 by and at the residence of Rev. J.L. Whitley in Mauk, Georgia.

**John T Lunsford**
Birth:
May 4, 1884
Death:
Oct. 27, 1940
Burial:
Mothers Home Cemetery
Miller County, Georgia

He was an early minister in the Martin Association.

**Levi B. Manning**
Birth:
Dec., 1879
Death:
1956
Burial:
Manningtown Presbyterian Cemetery
Manningtown
Wayne County, Georgia

Early minister in the South Georgia Association.

**Charles Courtney Martin**
Birth:
Mar. 9, 1827
Jasper County, Georgia
Death:
Nov. 25, 1910
Randolph County, Georgia
Burial:
Martin Family Cemetery
Randolph County, Georgia

He was one of six brothers, four of whom were preachers of the gospel. He united with the Free Will Baptist when 14 years of age; received license to preach at 21 and was ordained when 22. At this time many of the churches of his vicinity united with the larger Baptist body, but brother Martin remained faithful to the smaller denomination. He went to work seriously and incessantly to propagate a free salvation and his labors were blessed of God to the saving of many. He assisted in the organizing of numerous churches and two associations, one named the Martin Assn., and baptized 1531 converts. For more than 30 years he was a pastor of two churches in the Chattahoochee Association. His father was James Martin.

**George Washington Martin**
BIRTH
3 Jan 1829
Randolph County, Georgia, USA
DEATH
24 Oct 1915 (aged 86)
BURIAL
Martin Family Cemetery
Randolph County, Georgia, USA

**Son of James Martin & Hester Bogan also buried here-husband of Sarah Bradley buried beside him. Grave says George W Martin.**

Union, SC, and she is beside him. Many other family member in the cemetery." He stood in his integrity just and firm of purpose, Aiding Many, fearing none, a spectacle to Angels, and to men. Yea, when the shattered globe shall rock in the throes of dissolution, Still will he stand in his integrity, sublime, an honest man. (His epitath original poem By M F Tupper- From the "Cyclopaedia Of Poetry Embracing The Best From All Sources And On All Subjects" by Rev. Elon Foster. DD. pg 359)

### Robert M Massey
Birth:
Jun. 6, 1872
Death:
Nov. 26, 1966
Burial:
Oak Ridge Cemetery
Tifton
Tift County, Georgia
Plot: Annex III

He pastored in the Chattahoochee, Little River, and Union associations from about 1925 until 1946.

### James Martin
BIRTH
15 Nov 1788
Charleston, Charleston County, South Carolina, USA

DEATH
22 Nov 1869 (aged 81)
Randolph County, Georgia, USA

BURIAL
Martin Family Cemetery
Randolph County, Georgia, USA

Son of Robert Martin & Agnes Nancy LindseyHe married his wife Hester Bogan 31 Dec 1811

### Newton Elmore Massey

Birth:
Aug. 25, 1850
Muscogee County, Georgia
Death:
Nov. 3, 1914
Worth County, Georgia
Burial:
Hillcrest Cemetery
Sylvester
Worth County, Georgia

He was a minister in the Chattahoochee Association where records show that he was a pastor in 1892 through 1903. He was married to Julia Hill Massey (1850 - 1926) and they had two Children: Newton Elmore Massey (1878 - 1947) and Emma Massey Heath (1882 - 1952).

### Jordan B. McCullers

Birth
May 30, 1831
Dooley County, Georgia
Death:
Nov. 22, 1887
Burial:
Hodges Cemetery
Jakin,Early County, Georgia

He was converted in 1852, licensed in 1868, and ordained in April, 1874 by Bishop Pierce of the Methodists denomination. Since uniting with the Free Baptists his ministry has been in the Chattahoochee and Martin Associations baptizing over 100 converts and organized four

churches, one of them in Thomas County, Georgia while laboring as a missionary.

Inscription:
Confederate Memorials. D32 Ga. Inf. C.S.A.

### Solomon Oscar McCorvey

Birth:
Mar. 31, 1879
Death:
Oct. 30, 1955
Burial:
Oak Ridge Cemetery
Tifton
Tift County, Georgia
Plot: Annex III

The Liberty minutes show that he was recorded in the 1926 edition as a minister.

### Frank Steely McDanal

Birth:
Aug. 9, 1914
Death:
Jun. 21, 1966

Burial:
Parkhill Cemetery
Columbus
Muscogee County, Georgia

He was a minister in the Chattahoochee Association.

### John D McDaniel
Birth:
May 28, 1879
Death:
Jun. 24, 1947
Burial:
Satilla Freewill Baptist Church
Cemetery
Hazlehurst
Jeff Davis County, Georgia

He was in the Ogeechee Association.

### Walter Ballenger McDaniel
Birth:
Feb. 6, 1875
Death:
Mar. 1, 1931
Burial:
Oak Grove Cemetery
Americus
Sumter County, Georgia
Walter married Willie Adkins on 10 AUG 1902. He served as a minister in the Chattahoochee and Union Associations.

Inscription:
An Honest man is the noblest work of God

### Warren Arthur McDonald
Birth:
Dec. 25, 1848
Death:
Jul. 28, 1933
Burial:
Shepard Cemetery,
Miller County, Georgia

Rev. McDonald started several churches in the area, was quite prominent in his community and was a surveyor in Miller County as well. An old newspaper article concerning him stated there had been some stealing going on in the community; pigs, chickens, and homes entered and pilfered. No one knew who was doing it and could not seem to catch the thieves. One Sunday after church, Warren was going home in the mule and wagon. Suddenly, two unknown men jumped from the ditch bank and tried to hold him up. They apparently believed he would have the Sunday offering money with him. He told them to allow him to get it out of his inside coat pocket. He reached into the pocket, came out with a pistol instead, and shot and killed both men. He then left them lying there while he went to town and got the sheriff. He had no charges filed against him, and the stealing in the area stopped.

### Richard B. McFadden, Jr
Birth:
Mar. 17, 1951
Death:
Jul. 12, 2008
Burial:
Macon Memorial Park
Macon, Bibb County, Georgia

He ministered in the Georgia Union Association

### Peter McLain
Birth:
Nov. 19, 1843
Death:
Oct. 27, 1939
Burial:
New Hope Free Will Baptist
Church Cemetery
Madray Springs
Wayne County, Georgia

He was a minister in the Ogeechee and South Georgia Associations between 1903 and 1941 being recorded in the minutes of both associations on a regular basis.

### Seab A McLendon
Birth:
May 29, 1857
Death:
Nov. 25, 1942
Burial:
New Salem Cemetery
Miller County, Georgia

The Martin Association minutes from 1892 to 1921 record him as a minister.

**Clarence McMillan**
Birth:
Jul. 14, 1920
Death:
Dec. 19, 1994
Burial:
Sardis Cemetery
Folkston
Charlton County, Georgia

He was a minister in the South Georgia and Little River associations and whose record is found in the 1955 through 1988 minutes.He was married to the Leona Mock McMillan (1924 - 2011).

**Thomas B. Mellette**
Birth:
Apr. 25, 1892
Death:
Oct. 31, 1962
Burial:
Sowhatchee Cemetery,
Blakely
Early County,Georgia

He was one of the first educators in the early days of the denomination, who created Zion Bible School near Blakely. Mellette, who held degrees from several schools, including Columbia Bible College in Columbia, South Carolina, Zion served as the training ground for numerous ministers in Georgia, Florida, and Alabama. Many Zion graduates went on to become leaders in the national association. In 1942, after the national association established the Free Will Baptist Bible College in Nashville, Tennessee, Zion closed its doors and donated all its assets to the new school. He had been on the joint Education Committee that had been working together for the purpose of establishing a Free Will Baptist school. Mellette was from the Eastern General Conference.

**Henry Mills**
Birth:
Dec. 28, 1908
Death:
Dec. 20, 1988
Burial:
Oakland Cemetery
Waycross
Ware County, Georgia
Plot: Section K Lot 9C

Minister in the South Georgia Association.

### Cecil C Mock
Birth:
Oct. 25, 1917
Death:
Feb. 27, 1983
Burial:
Corinth Cemetery
Iron City
Seminole County, Georgia

He was a minister in the Martin Association. He was the son of John Henry Mock (1893 - 1966) and Alma Womble Mock (1898 - 1961).

---

### H. S. "Monty" Montgomery
Birth:
1919
Death:
1973
Burial:
Carroll Memory Gardens
Carrollton
Carroll County, Georgia
Plot: Sec 3, Row 11

He was a member of the Chattahoochee Association.

---

### Donald W. Moore
Birth:

May 24, 1919
Dodge County, Georgia
Death:
Oct. 12, 2002
Bibb County, Georgia
Burial:
Bay Springs Free Will Baptist
Church Cemetery
Plainfield, Dodge County,
Georgia

He was a minister in the Georgia Union Association. His parents were Jim Moore and Mary Hogan. He was married on July 14, 1941 in Dodge County to Ruby Lee Horne Moore (1913 - 2006) Service Info.: S1 US NAVY WORLD WAR II.

## Isaac Frank Musgrove
Birth:
Sep. 11, 1890
Death:
Aug. 20, 1967
Burial:
Liberty Hill Baptist Church
Cemetery
Hartsfield
Colquitt County, Georgia

Was a member of the Martin Association.

## Franklin "Seab" Myers
Birth:
Oct. 28, 1846
Gordon
Wilkinson County, Georgia
Death:
Feb. 8, 1911
Douglas
Coffee County, Georgia
Burial:
Carver Baptist Church Cemetery
Douglas
Coffee County, Georgia

He was the son of David and Mary Myers in Gordon, Wilkinson county Ga. On 09, July 1861 He along with Brother William, enlisted in Co. "B" 14th Ga Infantry Regiment CSA. They were joined later by their two brothers, John, and Daniel. William, John, and Daniel were all released before war end from illness, or wounds sustained in battle. But Seab served till surrender at Appomattox Courthouse, Virginia on April 09, 1865. He had been captured a month earlier, on March 25, near Petersburg Va, and was released on May 15th, at Point Lookout Maryland. He returned to Ga, and Married Susanna (Susan) Hersey on March 21, 1872 in Coffee county. His grave is marked with a confederate stone. Susan died at her daughter Ida's home in Perry, Taylor county Florida, and is buried in that county at New Hope cemetery. Her gravestone reads, Susan wife of S.F Myers Dec 22 1849-April-6-1918 having finished life's duty, she now sweetly rest. He was a member of the South Georgia conference.

## William T. Park
Birth:
Oct. 30, 1830
Death:
Sep. 6, 1919
Burial:
Boynton Cemetery
Catoosa County,
Georgia
Plot: Row 6

He was an early minister in the Chattahoochee Association and is recorded in the 1848 minutes of that conference.
Inscription:
2nd Co. "D", Ist Ga Inf., C.S.A.

**William H. Parkman**
Birth:
Jan. 8, 1831
Death:
May 7, 1907
Burial:
Fort Benning Cemetery #02
Fort Benning
Chattahoochee County,
Georgia

In the 1848 minutes of the Chattahoochee Association listed as a minister. Confederate Civil War Veteran. 1850 Census McNorton's, Muscogee Co GA. Film M432_79 pg 403A in household with his parents, John and Susan V. A Parkman and a lot of siblings. U.S. Civil War Soldier Records and Profiles Name: William Parkman Residence: Muscogee County, Georgia Enlistment Date: 5 Dec 1862 Rank at enlistment: Private State Served: Georgia Survived the War: Service Record: Enlisted in Pemberton's Company G, Georgia 54th Infantry Regiment on 16 May 1862. Mustered out on 25 May 1862 at Savannah, GA.

Sources: Roster of Confederate Soldiers of Georgia 1861-1865. C. L. Torbett Funeral Home, Columbus, GA Funeral Services Billed for May 7, 1907 $28.00.

**Neal H Parrish**
Birth:
Jul. 13, 1880
Death:
Sep. 6, 1962
Burial:
Friendship Cemetery
Hahira,Lowndes County, Georgia

Records revealed in four different associations that he pastored or was a minister there in. Namely; South Georgia, Georgia Union, Little River and Union Associations.

**Oliver Hazard John Perry**
Birth:
Jan. 7, 1865
Death:
Mar. 14, 1942
Burial:
Cedar Springs Cemetery
Cedar Springs
Early County, Georgia

He was an early minister in the Martin and Midway Association at the turn-of-the-century from 1902 until 1926.

### August Jonathan Peters
Birth:
Dec. 5, 1847
Death:
Aug. 31, 1917
Burial:
Jesup City Cemetery
Jesup
Wayne County, Georgia

The minutes of the Martin Association record him in the 1893 edition. Then he is found in 1902 in the Midway Association.

### James L Pittman
Birth:
Mar. 27, 1892
Death:
Jan. 22, 1977
Burial:
Smyrna Baptist Church Cemetery
Deepstep, Washington County, Georgia
A record of him is found in 1961 Chattahoochee minutes.

### Roscoe Pitts
Birth:
Feb. 23, 1923
Georgia
Death:
Nov. 2, 1994
Columbus
Muscogee County, Georgia
Burial:
Riverdale Cemetery
Columbus
Muscogee County, Georgia

Roscoe was married to Avie Lou Howard. He was a preacher in the Chattahoochee and Georgia Union Association's ranging from about 1955 until 1987. He is recorded numerous times in these record books.

**James Monroe Posey**
Birth:
Mar. 5, 1852
Taylor County, Georgia
Death:
Aug. 1, 1918
Burial:
New Prospect Free Will Baptist
Church Cemetery, Reynolds
Taylor County, Georgia
His name is recorded in the Chattahoochee mintues from 1885 until 1917 in most all editions.

**James L Poston**
Birth:
Jul. 7, 1881
Death:
Jul. 20, 1952
Burial:
Pine Level Freewill Baptist
Church Cemetery
Chester
Dodge County, Georgia
His ministry was confined to the Georgia Union Association.
Spouse: Eunice T Poston (1889 - 1982)

**James W. Potter**
Birth:
Aug. 15, 1931
Death:
Jan. 24, 1991
Burial:
Middle Georgia Memory Gardens
Jones County, Georgia

He ministered in three Georgia associations. Namely; South Georgia, Chattahoochee and Georgia Union Associations.

### William S Powell
Birth:
Jul. 24, 1875, USA
Death:
Mar. 13, 1932
Georgia
Burial:
Satilla Freewill Baptist Church
Cemetery
Hazlehurst, Jeff Davis, Georgia

He was an early minister in the South Georgia conference whose name is recorded in the 1929 and 1931 minutes.

### William L Presley
Birth:
Apr. 8, 1820
Death:
Aug. 31, 1887
Burial:
Mount Zion Baptist Church
Cemetery
Towns County, Georgia

He is a minister whose name appears in the Chattahoochee minutes of 1842, 1847 and 1848.

### William Lester Purvis
Georgia Birth:
Feb. 20, 1899
Death:
Aug. 8, 1979
Burial:
Purvis Cemetery
Coffee County, Georgia

He preached in a number of conferences in Georgia, namely; South Georgia, Georgia Union, Chattahoochee, Union and Little River Conferences.

### Calvin C Quinn
Birth:
Jan. 3, 1870
Death:
Dec. 13, 1942
Burial:
Satilla Freewill Baptist Church
Cemetery
Hazlehurst
Jeff Davis County, Georgia

He preached in the South Georgia conference and his name appears in the 1907 minutes. He was married to Rebecca A Bland Quinn (1893 - 1927) and they had two children: Alvin H and Esther Lee.

**Henry Smith Reese**
Birth:
Nov. 21, 1827
Jasper County, Georgia
Death:
Nov. 11, 1922
Turin
Coweta County, Georgia
Burial:
Tranquil Cemetery
Coweta County, Georgia

He is in the 1848 minutes of the Chattahooche Assn. He was a twin brother of John Palmer Reese. He was the son of Reverend James Reese and Rebecca (Smith) Reese. He was an ordained Baptist minister despite his lack of a formal education as well as a prominent writer and singer of Sacred Harp music. His ministry covered almost seventy years at churches throughout Georgia. In 1857, he married Amanda Brawner and this union produced one daughter. In 1865, he married a widow, Martha Jane (Leavell) Brooks, and there were seven children born of this union. He was also a teacher of Sacred Harp music according to the Baptist Biography (1920).

19 Sep 1891
Muscogee County, Georgia.

BURIAL
Pierce Chapel Unite
Methodist Church Cemetery
Harris County, Georgia.

He was a close associate of Cyru
White founder of the
Chattahoochee United Baptis
Association especially during his
years in Alabama. He appears in th
1842 Chattahoochee minutes as
minister representing the Smyrn
church in Russell County, Alabamɛ
He later aligns himself with th
churches of Christ with th
restoration movement..

**Rev James Ree**

BIRTH
12 Jul 1801
Edgefield County, South Carolina.

DEATH

DEATH
13 May 1900 (aged 72)
Newnan, Coweta County,
Georgia, USA

BURIAL
Oak Hill Cemetery
Newnan, Coweta County,
Georgia,

Squire J. P. Reese, The Herald Correspon-
dent "Ripples"

**John Palmer Reese**

BIRTH
23 Nov 1827
Jasper County, Georgia, USA

Twin brother of Henry Smith
Rees. He was the son of Reverend
James Rees and Rebecca (Smith)
Rees. He served in Company I of
the 37th Georgia Infantry during
the Civil War. He married
Elizabeth Mosley (date
unknown) of which there were
ten children born to this union.
He was a prominent writer and
singer of Sacred Harp music and
taught singing schools for a

number of years in Georgia and Alabama. He served for a time as the president of the Chattahoochie Music Association and the Chattahoochie Convention and was a major contributor to the 1859 Sacred Harp revision.

Records show that on August 20, 1827 he preached at the Macedonia Baptist Church near Newman Georgia with the Rev. Cyrus white. His brother H. C. Closely associated with Cyrus white often living near him. James appears in the Chattahoochee minutes for 1848 and as J. P. In 1851 as a licensed. He wrote a column in the Newman, Georgia Hererd which led to his nickname ripples.

**C D Rentz**
Birth:
May 7, 1916
Death:
Jun. 22, 2001
Burial:
Memorial Freewill
Baptist Church Cemetery
Surrency
Appling County, Georgia

He is recorded many times in the South Georgia and Georgia Union conferences.

**Charlie T Rentz**
Birth:
1894
Death:
1952
Burial:
Westview Cemetery
Moultrie
Colquitt County, Georgia
Plot: Lane 10 East; Section 6,
Block C, Lot 45 (6 C 45 10th
East)

He was a minister in the Union Conference.
Inscription:
RENTZ Rev. Charlie T.
Rentz 1894 ----- 1952
At Rest

**Wilbur L Rentz**
Birth:
Nov. 16, 1923
Death:
Aug. 29, 2007
Burial:
Memorial Freewill Baptist
Church Cemetery
Surrency
Appling County, Georgia


He was a preacher in the Midway and Martin conferences

**G W Rhodes**
Birth:
Mar. 6, 1870
Death:
Mar. 9, 1941
Burial:
Bethlehem Schley Baptist
Church Cemetery, Moultrie
Colquitt County, Georgia

He was a preacher in the Union Association.

**Charles W Rickerson**
Birth:
1868
Death:
1930
Burial:
Oak Ridge Cemetery
Tifton
Tift County, Georgia
Plot: old sect. blk 21, lot 4;
C W Rickerson plot
He was a preacher in the Chattahoochee Association.

**Bill Robinson**
Birth:
Apr. 11, 1927,
Liberty, Tennessee
Death:
May 13, 2005
Bainbridge, Georgia

Burial:
Mount Gilead
Freewill Baptist Church
Cemetery, Brinston,
Decatur County,Georgia

He was a United States Navy veteran of World War II and a 1962 graduate of Free Will Baptist Bible college in Nashville Tennessee. He was very active in denominational affairs and served for 12 years on the Board of Trustees of Free Will Baptist Bible College. He pastored churches in Tennessee, Michigan, Mississippi, North Carolina and Georgia. He retired as a Minister after 45 years of service and his retirement was only because of his health. He had diabetes for 35 years, had an open heart surgery, and only months before his death he lost a leg. He also had a brother of whom he was proud, Paul Robinson, who was a Free Will Baptist missionary to Uruguay.

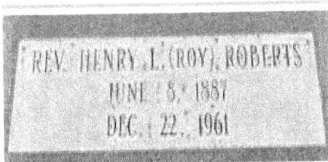

**Henry Leroy "Roy" Roberts**
Birth:
Jun. 8, 1887
Miller County, Georgia
Death:
Dec. 22, 1961
Miller County, Georgia
Burial:
Primitive Union Cemetery
Colquitt

Miller County, Georgia

He was a minister in the Martin and Midway conferences between the years of 1921 until 1959 according to the minutes of both associations.

**Harris Edgar Rogers**
Birth:
Aug. 13, 1888
Death:
Feb. 3, 1969
Burial:
Roberta City Cemetery
Roberta
Crawford County, Georgia
Plot: 351B

He is recorded as a minister in the Union minutes in 1952.

### Eugene F. Ross
Birth:
Sep. 10, 1933
Dodge County, Georgia
Death:
Nov. 1, 2009
Cochran
Bleckley County, Georgia
Burial:
Bethany Baptist Church
Cemetery
Bleckley County, Georgia

His ministry is recorded in the Georgia Union, Union and Chattahoochee minutes.

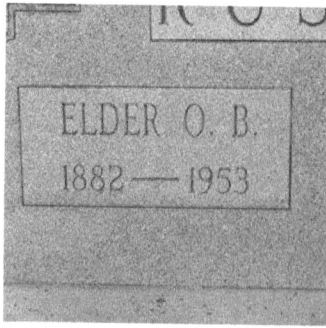

### Elder Osceola Butler Rustin
BIRTH
1882
DEATH
1953 (aged 70–71)
BURIAL
Eastside Cemetery
Statesboro,
Bulloch County,
Georgia

He officiated the funeral for Dr. Eugene L. St. Claire, GA, in 1916.

### Vester Sadler
Birth:
Aug. 31, 1934
Death:
Jan. 13, 2007
Burial:
New Hope Cemetery
Cairo
Grady County, Georgia

Minister in Martin Association.

### Pete Allen Sangster
Birth:
Jun. 12, 1872
Dooly Co, GA
Death:
Dec. 20, 1944
Burial:
Blackshear City Cemetery
Blackshear
Pierce County,
Georgia

He was a minister in the Georgia Union conference.

### Leon L. Sapp, Jr.
Birth:
Jan. 2, 1928
Death:

Oct. 13, 1974
Burial:
Lone Hill Cemetery
Coffee County,
Georgia

He was a preacher in the following four conferences; Chattahoochee, Georgia Union, South Georgia and Union conferences. He was married to Heloyse Turner Sapp.

**Joseph Washington Sauls**
Birth:
Oct. 18, 1847
Death:
Mar. 7, 1919
Burial:
Bethlehem Freewill
Baptist Church Cemetery
Shellman
Randolph County,
Georgia

Brother Saul's was born and reared in Randolph County, and there he spent his entire life and raised a large and useful family. He became converted, joined the church, was baptized and soon afterwards began to preach and was ordained as a minister of the Gospel, and served a number of churches in the Bethel Association. In his own home church and community he was most useful. The lives of such men as this are jewels and they become the very foundation of the church and community life wherever they live. He and some of his family migrated from NC to Georgia..

**Kenneth V. Shutes**
Birth:
Jul. 9, 1905
Death:
Dec. 18, 1962
Burial:
Floral Memory Gardens,
Albany,
Dougherty County,
Georgia

Shutes for many years directed the Superannuation Board, which administered an insurance program for full-time ministers in the denomination.

**Dr. Eugene Louis St. Claire**
Birth:
Jun. 9, 1865,
Georgia
Death:
Feb. 6, 1916,
Florida
Burial:
Ebenezer Cemetery, Glennville,
Tattnall County, Georgia

Prominent evangelist of the Free Will Baptist denomination. At the time of his death, not yet 50 years old, he was living in Live Oak, FL, trying to regain his health following several paralytic strokes. Dr. St. Claire had been pastoring the church in Glennville, GA, and his body was returned for burial in the Ebenezer F.W.B. cemetery. Reverend O. B. Rustin officiated at his funeral. An account of his death appeared in the *Free Will Baptist* published. In Ayden, North Carolina. On Feb. 16, 1916, with a tribute to his life and ministry. Editor Phillips stated, "Dr. St. Claire, had conducted many revival campaigns there and had won many friends by his kind and genial disposition. Especially was he remembered for the great zeal and energy he had put in building and strengthening the Free Will Baptist Seminary in Ayden, N.C.

He was orphaned at age four years, and it is unknown if he had any siblings. Both parents were of French descent according to the 1900 U.S. Census. He spent his early life on an old-fashioned plantation. He pursued his higher education at the University of Alabama, with Master of Arts, and in one paper, the editor states he studied and graduated from "several theological colleges."

The Doctor of Divinity designation appears wherever his name appears in print. Upon completing his secular education, he embarked upon a successful business career, but soon felt the call to the ministry. In his relatively short period of twenty-three years of ministry, his accomplishments were nothing short of phenomenal. In several of our Southern states he has done a great work. Association after association has been organized and put in working order. Thousands of souls have been led to the Lord in his meetings. In his first year of ministry, he helped to organize three associations. In his autobiography, he stated he organized 73 churches and won and baptized 4,879 persons.

FWB church records at Glennville, show that Dr. St. Claire was its founder in the year 1899. He pastored this church off and on up until his death.

Dr. St. Claire was also known as an orator, writer, and public debater. Debating was one of his skills, done in a witty manner, and at least five of these occasions are on record. He is acclaimed as one of the foremost preachers of the land, of scholarly ability, a man of culture and zeal, and service to his denomination.

For Dr. St. Claire's entire life as a Christian and as a minister of the Gospel, he was almost totally blind. This would mean that his Bible and theological education was acquired in spite of his lack of physical vision. How he acquired such vast and thorough knowledge of letters is hard to imagine for that time. However it came to him, he got it. This is a tribute to his indomitable spirit, for such a man cannot be defeated. His wife died shortly before he did. [It is unknown where she is buried]

**Tombstone of Dr. St. Claire**

**Linza D Scott**
Birth:
Mar. 29, 1896, USA
Death:
Aug. 22, 1977, USA
Burial:
Brinson Cemetery
Brinson
Decatur County, Georgia
He was a minister in the Martin conference according to its minutes from about 1943 until 1975.

**Farest W Sellers**
Birth:
May 26, 1912
Death:
Jun. 16, 1984
Burial:
Branchville United Methodist
Church Cemetery
Camilla,
Mitchell County, Georgia

He pastored in the Martin, Union and Ogeechee conferences according to the minutes of all three conferences beginning in 1946 until 1983.

**James Robert Sellers**
Birth:
May 12, 1925
Toombs County, Georgia
Death:
December 6, 2019
Archbold Memorial Hospital
Moultrie, Georgia
Burial:
Cobb Suncrest Memory Gardens
Moultrie, Georgia

He was born the son of the late Atha Matilda Sellers and Fred Robert Sellers. He retired from Swift and Company as a supervisor in the beef dressing department and was a Free Will Baptist minister pastoring several churches in the Moultrie area.

**Willie A. Sellers**
Birth:
Jan. 23, 1881
Death:
Jul. 14, 1975
Burial:
Branchville United Methodist
Church Cemetery
Camilla
Mitchell County, Georgia

He pastored in the Liberty, Union and Martin conferences according to the records of all three beginning in 1926 and continuing until 1969.

### Rev Seaborne G. Smith
Birth
25 Feb 1846
Death
25 Sep 1926
Burial
Satilla Freewill Baptist Church
Cemetery
Hazlehurst,
Jeff Davis County, Georgia,

He was a brother-in-law to James Alfred Ray, the father-in-law of Dr. Eugene Louis St. Claire.

### Thomas J. Strickland
Birth:
Aug. 1, 1861
Tattnall County, Georgia
Death:
Mar. 18, 1920
Wayne County, Georgia
Burial:
Hopewell Methodist Church
Cemetery
Tattnall County, Georgia
He is found in the Ogeechee minutes in 1903 and later in the South Georgia 1905-1911. He was married to Caroline Surrency.

### James R. Stroup
Birth:
Nov. 16, 1914
Death:
Jun. 29, 1987
Burial:
Middle Georgia Memory Gardens
Jones County, Georgia
He was a minister in the Chattahoochee and Georgia Union Associations.

### Grover Cleveland Sullivan
Birth:
Oct. 31, 1893
Dooly County, Georgia
Death:
Jan. 27, 1986
Perry
Houston County, Georgia
Burial:
Snow Methodist Church
Cemetery
Unadilla
Dooly County, Georgia
Was a minister in Georgia Union Association.

### John Taylor
Birth:
Feb. 14, 1818
Emanuel County, Georgia
Death:
Jan. 12, 1896
Worth County, Georgia
Burial:
Old Shiloh Cemetery
Tift County, Georgia

He was a clergyman in the Chattahoochee Assn according to its minutes in 1891-92.

### J. L. Tedder
Birth:
Jul. 18, 1886
Death:
Dec. 6, 1960
Burial:
Sowhatchee Cemetery
Blakely
Early County, Georgia

From 1923 until 1960 he was a minister in the Midway and Martin Associations.

### James Alfred Thompson
Birth:
Sep., 1849
Appling Co, Georgia

Death:
1910
Burial:
Bethel Free Will Baptist Church Cemetery
Appling County, Georgia

He preached in the Ogeechee and South Georgia associations in the early part of the 1900s.

### Allen L Thornton
Birth:
Dec. 5, 1872
Death:
May 18, 1953
Burial:
Satilla Freewill Baptist Church Cemetery
Hazlehurst
Jeff Davis County, Georgia

He was a preacher in the South Georgia Association and is recorded in most of the minutes from 1919 until 1953.

### A J Tomlinson
Birth:
Aug. 6, 1870
Death:
Mar. 18, 1951
Burial:
Pine Level Cemetery
Cairo
Grady County, Georgia

He was a minister in the Liberty and Martin associations from 1921 until 1950.

### Moutrie H Touchton
Birth:
Aug. 22, 1876
Death:
Feb. 3, 1961
Burial:
Boney Bluff Cemetery
Echols County, Georgia

He was a preacher in the Little River Association.

### Thomas J. Touchton
Birth:
Sep. 28, 1905
Death:
Jul. 15, 1907
Burial:
Macedonia Baptist Church Cemetery
Mayday
Echols County,
Georgia

He was a minister in the Union Association.

### Willie Gus Turner
Birth:
Jun. 29, 1922
Sale City
Mitchell County,
Georgia
Death:
Aug. 9, 2012
Cairo
Grady County, Georgia
Burial:
Carter-Banks Cemetery
Grady County, Georgia

Rev. Turner was born to the late David Glenn Turner and Blanchie M. Johnson Turner. On March 23, 1946, he married Nancy Elizabeth Banks Turner. Rev. Turner was a minister for 66 years (32 years at First Freewill of Cairo, Georgia). He served his country in the U. S. Army, as an honorable veteran, fighting on the front line in the European Theatre of WWII. His ministry was spent in the Martin and Union associations.

### James Edward Usury
Birth:
May 6, 1935
Graham, Appling County,
Georgia
Death:
Mar. 16, 2013
Jeff Davis County,
Georgia
Burial:
Satilla Freewill Baptist Church Cemetery
Hazlehurst, Jeff Davis County,
Georgia

He graduated from Jeff Davis high school. He desired for education and took correspondence courses after graduation, including some courses from Welch College (then Free Will Baptist Bible College). After graduation from High School he worked at a news agency. He married Janice Quinn who was a real asset and blessing in his Christian Ministry. James was called to the ministry at the age of 21 and was ordained the next year. He was ordained in the South Georgia Association and those serving on the Ordaining Committee were: Dr. Tom Hamilton, Dr. Ralph Lightsey and Rev. C. D. Rentz. His first pastorate was at the Oak Hill Church and then at the Corinth Church both in the South Georgia Association. In 1967 he was called to the Midway Church, Moultrie, in the Union Association and was there until 1976. The Lord led him to the First Church in Columbus, Twin Cities Association until 1982. Then they went back to the South Georgia Association, First Church in Jessup until 1990. He then served the New Home Church in the Martin Association until 1999 when he officially retired from active ministry because of health problems and went back home to Hazlehurst. During his ministry there were at least five young men called to ministry: Rev. Steve Hughes, Dr. Billy Lewis, Rev. Irvin Murphy, Rev. Ken Murphy and Rev. Curtis Alligood. James was totally involved in Free Will Baptist ministry. In the districts where he pastured he served in various capacities including committees and moderator. At the State level, he was on the Resolution Committee; served as music director for the State Meeting; served on Board of Christian Education; Budgeting Committee; was Chairman of the Board of Mission and in 1985 was elected Clerk of the State. Officiating the services were Rev. Paul Smith, Rev. Herbert Waid and Rev. Steve Hughes.

---

### Julian Vickers
Birth:
Dec. 20, 1923
Death:
Mar. 27, 2002
Burial:
Hebron Cemetery
Coffee County, Georgia

He preached in the Union and Little River associations.

He was a preacher in the Martin Association.

**Edgar Jackson Wade**
Birth:
Jan. 1, 1881
Georgia
Death:
Jan. 11, 1952
Cordele
Crisp County, Georgia
Burial:
Sunnyside Cemetery
Cordele
Crisp County, Georgia

He preached in the Georgia Union conference.

**Frank W Wade**
Birth:
Feb. 22, 1884
Death:
Nov. 12, 1954
Burial:
Colquitt City Cemetery
Colquitt
Miller County, Georgia

**Samuel Watkins, Jr**
Birth:
1779
Richland County, South Carolina
Death:
Apr. 15, 1855
Columbus
Muscogee County, Georgia
Burial:
New Providence Baptist Church Cemetery
Muscogee County, Georgia

Rev. Samuel Watkins, Jr. was the son of Samuel Watkins, Sr, and Elizabeth (unknown). He married Charity (unknown) about 1808 in Richland Co., SC and they were the parents of six children: William, Zachariah, Samuel, Ervin, Epsey and George Washington Watkins. He migrated from Richland Co., SC to Muscogee Co., GA about 1833. He was an early pastor of the New Providence Freewill Baptist Church. The dates for Samuel and Charity were accidently reversed on the tombstone.

**Benjamin Blanton Watson**
Birth:
Aug. 24, 1829
Marion County, Georgia
Death:
Feb. 13, 1915
Taylor County, Georgia
Burial:
Trinity Freewill Baptist
Cemetery
Taylor County, Georgia

The 1842 Chattahoochee Assn minutes record him as a minister. He was the son of Richard William Ansley Watson (1803 - 1871) and Sealia R Waller Watson (1802 - 1870). He married Sarah Frances Rebecca Lawhorn Watson (1834 - 1921).

**John R. Weeks**
Birth:
Apr. 24, 1891
Death:
Dec. 30, 1947
Burial:
Weeks Chapel Cemetery
Norman Park
Colquit County, Georgia

He was a minister in the Little River conference.

**John B Wheeler**
Birth:
Sep. 29, 1875
Death:
Mar. 13, 1967
Burial:
Oak Ridge Cemetery
Tifton
Tift County,
Georgia

He preached in both the Little River and South Georgia conferences.

**Connie C White**
Birth:
Oct. 27, 1878
Death:
May 22, 1975
Burial:
White Plains Freewill Baptist Church Cemetery
Lucile
Early County,
Georgia

Son of Andrew Jackson White (buried at Blakely City Cemetery) and Linton Ann Malinda Mills White. Married Ola Barbrie on 17 Aug 1899 in Early County, Georgia. The minutes of the Midway Association beginning in 1916 record him in most all minutes until 1971.
Inscription:
In thee o Lord have I put my trust

**A. G. Windham**
Birth:
Jul. 19, 1927
Death:
Jul. 22, 2014
Reynolds, Taylor County, Georgia
Burial:
Mount Olive Freewill Baptist Church Cemetery
Potterville, Taylor County, Georgia

He was a member of Mt. Olive Free Will Baptist Church and for over 43 years he had pastored several churches in the Chattahoochee Association of Free Will Baptists, including Little Bethel, Turners Chapel, Mt. Olive, Spring Hill and New Liberty. He retired from Robins Air Force Base after 31 years. He served in WW II as a merchant Marine.

**James L. "Jim" Whitley**
Birth:
Mar. 11, 1883
Death:
Sep. 5, 1968
Burial:
Pine Level Cemetery
Mauk, Taylor County, Georgia

He was a minister in the Chattahoochee Association. He was the son of James M. and Polly Whitley, who married Fannie Lucinda Lee Hayes Whitley (1882 - 1956).

**L B Whitley**
Birth:
1855
Death:
1929
Burial:
Brushy Creek Cemetery
Adel,Cook County, Georgia

He is recorded in the Liberty minutes in 1895.

**Green Thomas Wiley**
Birth:
Apr. 10, 1845
Death:
Sep. 14, 1917
Burial:
Sowhatchee Cemetery
Blakely
Early County, Georgia
His ministry began in 1879 in the Chattahoochee Association where he served until 1885. Afterwards, he joined the Martin Association in 1892 and remained there until 1902. He joined the Midway Association in 1902 and served there until 1909. He was the husband of Margaret (Walter) Wiley and son of Jacob Wiley,Jr and Mary D. (Lane) Wiley.

**William T Wiley**
Birth:
Sep. 6, 1868
Georgia
Death:
Jun. 26, 1952
Burial:
Sowhatchee Cemetery
Blakely
Early County, Georgia

He joined the Martin Association in 1887 and in 1902 he united with the Midway Association and remained there until 1948 as a clergyman. He married Ella G. Alston Wiley (1873 - 1975).

**Samuel Longstreet Wilkinson**
Birth:
May 13, 1933
Death:
Apr. 11, 1988
Burial:
Ebenezer Cemetery
Glennville
Tattnall County, Georgia
Plot: Section B2

His name appears in the South Georgia minutes on a regular basis from 1954 until 1985. He was a Minister, Missionary in Brazil 19 years, and a professor at Hillsdale FWB College. Husband of Volree June Goode.
Inscription:
Children: Kevin, Kimberly, Kenan

**E. C. Williams**
Birth:
Jan. 8, 1879
Death:
Feb. 16, 1970
Burial:
New Enterprise Freewill Baptist Church Cemetery
Seminole County, Georgia

He served in the Midway and Martin Association's from 1919 until 1969. He was married to Abbie Rebecca Williams

(1887 - 1947) and to them had the following children; Infant Son William (1905 1905), Anderson Williams (1906 - 1971), Nita Williams Tyler (1907 - 1998), J. T. Williams (1913-1934) Modainer R. Williams (1914 - 1930).

### Kinnebrew Willis, Sr
Birth:
1812
Morgan County, Georgia
Death:
Dec. 12, 1880
Lee County,, Alabama
Burial:
Emmaus Baptist Church
Cemetery
Muscogee County, Georgia

His name appears in the Chattahoochee minutes of 1879. It is SPECULATIVE that this individual is buried at Emmaus Baptist Cemetery - at least two of his children, one who died during the Civil War in 1864 and another who died in 1934, are buried here. Said to be son of Robert L. Isabel (Frazier) Willis, Sr. Married ca. 1837, probably in Muscogee County, Georgia, to Nancy Motley. Father of fifteen children.

### Harvey J. Wilson
Birth:
Dec. 28, 1902
Death:
Aug. 24, 1932
Burial:
New Hope Free Will Baptist
Church Cemetery
Madray Springs
Wayne County,
Georgia

He was a member of the Union conference.

### Riley H Windham
Birth:
Feb. 12, 1908
Death:
Jun. 22, 1987
Burial:
Mount Olive Freewill Baptist
Church Cemetery
Potterville
Taylor County,
Georgia

The Chattahoochee minutes record him from 1930 until 1948.

### Needham Graham Yarbrough
Birth:
Nov. 28, 1842
Williamsburg County, South
Carolina
Death:
Mar. 10, 1928
Wayne County, Georgia
Burial:
George Cemetery
Wayne County, Georgia

Rev. Yarbrough's parents were: Needham Madison and Rebecca Wright Yarbrough. He enlisted in Clarendon County, South Carolina with Co. H 26th Regiment, South Carolina Volunteers along with his brothers John Edward, William, his brother in law John McCaskill and his uncle John Yarbrough during the War Between the States. Before the war he was working as a farm hand on the Jones farm in Clarendon, South Carolina where he met and fell in love with Eliza McCaskill. Family members said he came to the field one day and ask her to marry him and off they went to Charleston, SC and was married that very day Dec. 24, 1860. During the war his father Needham Madison Yarbrough went to South Carolina and brought his sons family to his home in Liberty Co., Georgia. After the war Needham G. moved his family from Georgia to Starke Florida. In a letter he wrote back to his father, he wrote it took 3 months by ox and cart to get there and they had to fight off Indians during the journey. Years later he and the family moved back to Georgia and settled in Wayne County, Georgia. The Ogeechee minutes showed him as a clergyman in their Association in 1903 and later the South Georgia minutes in 1905 through 1907 showed him as a minister.

**Thomas Patrick Young**
Birth:
Jan. 15, 1843
Death:
Dec. 18, 1908
Columbus
Muscogee County, Georgia
Burial:
Riverdale Cemetery
Columbus
Muscogee County, Georgia
Plot: Section 7, North
1/2 of Lot 93

Son of Marmaduke N.and Elizabeth (McSWAIN) YOUNG. The local newspaper said:."MR. T. P. YOUNG DIED YESTERDAY: Was 66 Years of Age and a Confederate Veteran--Funeral Tomorrow Morning. The deceased was a member of the Free Will Baptist church and was held in high esteem by all who knew him. The news of his death will bring sorrow to many homes in the community in which he lived. He was a gallant soldier in the service of the south during the civil war and the following page from an old family record bears out the fact of his loyalty to his state: Enlisted in Company B, Captain R. F. PARDY, (of Muscogee county) Thirty-first Georgia regiment, volunteers, October 4th, 1861. Was captured at Appomattox, Va., May 12th, 1864, carried to Fort Delaware. Paroled March 10th, 1865. During the war he served under Generals A. R. LAWTON, John B. GORDON, Clement A. EVANS, Jeb. A. EARLY, and a member of

JACKSON's corps, Army of Northern Virginia. Was wounded on the 13th of December, 1862, and afterwards joined the ranks.' Besides his devoted wife, he is survived by five children, as follows: Messrs. F. B. YOUNG, of Chattanooga; F. R. YOUNG, Jr., of the United States navy; W. L. YOUNG, C. L. YOUNG, of Columbus, and G. N. YOUNG, of Milledgeville. He is also survived by two brothers, Messrs. F. R. YOUNG, of Columbus, and O. C. YOUNG, of Girard. The funeral will take place tomorrow morning at ten o'clock from the late residence, and 'Taps' will be sounded over the grave by Messrs. Marion Schley DAVIS and Gurlin F. DAVIS, of the Columbus Guards." [Columbus (GA) Enquirer-Sun newspaper, Saturday, 19 DEC 1908, p. 3.]" Sunday morning at 10 o'clock, the services being conducted by the Rev. Mr. KIDD. The funeral was largely attended by relatives and friends of the deceased. Camp Benning was also represented at the funeral, as Mr. YOUNG was a member of the camp and served the south well during the civil war. Interment was in Riverdale cemetery and the following members of Camp Benning acted as pallbearers: Probably the most impressive feature of the ceremony at the grave was the sounding of 'taps' immediately after the services by Mr. Marion Schley DAVIS, leader of the Columbus Guards drum and bugle corps." [Columbus (GA) Enquirer-Sun newspaper, Tuesday, 22 DEC 1908, p. 8..Entry in Sexton's Card File for Riverdale Cemetery: